In the Armies
of the
Living God

A Novelette Set in the Scriptural
Knowledge of the End Times

Michael K. Pasque

See, the storm of the LORD will burst out in wrath, a driving wind swirling down on the heads of the wicked.

The fierce anger of the LORD will not turn back until he fully accomplishes the purposes of his heart. In days to come you will understand this.

—Jeremiah 30:23-24

Chapter 1

Eternity

My step into eternity is infinitely more than I ever anticipated. Those "close brush with death" reports, which had been so popularized by the media during my life, had not even come close. In the instant of my death, I slip quietly and immediately into that which they had been incapable of describing, the unveiled presence of God. Human language is so utterly inadequate to describe pure and infinite holiness. The totality of all that I had known during my life cannot comprehend what I experience in this moment of my death.

C.S. Lewis hit the nail right on the head. In this moment my reality has melted away. I am immediately in the palpable presence of the One who in fact stood beside me my whole life. My eyes, my entire consciousness, immediately focus on the image before me. But the word *image* is inadequate to describe what I now perceive. For the perception of God that completely engulfs me goes infinitely beyond the limited scope of human vision as I had once known it. It is in fact the exact experience, comprehension, and knowledge of God that I had sought, consciously and unconsciously, from the moment of my birth. Upon my death, I submerge into the depths of the ocean that is the infinity of God and, as if gasping for air, I frantically—uncontrollably—gulp in all that I can hold. In an instant it fills my mind and heart like the ocean filling the lungs of a drowning man. It overwhelms all of my senses.

For a single fleeting instant I stand in the presence of the full glory of the Mighty God. The full knowledge of the Most Holy One. Holiness as it can only be infinitely defined. Pure light. Pure justice. Pure love. All knowing. All powerful.

I stand clothed only in my naked decaying human body for barely the blink of an eye. It is only an instant, an immeasurably small increment of time. But in that almost timeless instant I know the totality of the measure of my depravity. In that instant I somehow know and live and understand the absolute darkness of every single moment of belligerent rebellion against the knowledge of God that was found in my heart since my childhood.

Then it occurs—something I had practiced repeatedly in my mind on many occasions during my life. It had occurred then only when the Spirit of the Living God had led me to true repentance and a full comprehension of my standing before an infinite, omnipotent, holy God. On those occasions I had, in my heart and in my mind, immediately lain prostrate before God. On the day that I gave my heart to Jesus Christ, when I had truly surrendered control of my life to my Lord and Redeemer, I had known this position as the only suitable position. For when I had humbly accepted the free gift of salvation found only in belief in the shed blood of the Lamb, no other position would suffice.

Now before God the Father, my submission occurs before I even have a chance to *will* it to happen. In an instant I lay face down before God. My salvation is now, as the Word had said, not based on my effort—for there is no time for any effort on my part. There is time only for Jesus, my Redeemer and resident of my heart, to throw me instantly to the ground—just in time to avoid the wrath of the Father. The Spirit of Jesus in my heart, the salvation as promised.

> *When I saw him, I fell at his feet as though dead.*
>
> —Revelation 1:17

In this instant of my salvation I fully understand the fate of those who do not surrender their hearts to Jesus during their life. They, like me, will stand before Almighty God clothed only in the filth of their inequity. They rely on their own efforts during their life and they will rely on their own efforts in the instant of their death.

> *This is the fate of those* <u>*who trust in themselves*</u> *... Like sheep they are destined for the grave, and death will feed on them. The upright will rule over them in the morning; their forms will decay in the grave, far from their princely mansions.*
>
> —Psalm 49:13-14 (emphasis added)

They rely on their good works, their talents, their abilities, their wealth, their fame, their worldly knowledge, and their wisdom during their lives, and they will have to rely on them then, too—for there is no Redeemer, no rescue, in their hearts.

And this will not be good enough. For in the full measure of their wickedness they will stand before the pure holiness of the Mighty God. And the Father, whose perfect justice is as undeniable as His perfect love, will instantly release the only possible response to rebellion against His holiness. He had told them this clearly—that He cannot help but guard His glory and His holiness—for such rebellion simply cannot stand. To allow otherwise would be to deny the very nature of God; if He could even allow otherwise, He simply would not be *God*.

> *"By myself I have sworn, my mouth has uttered in all integrity <u>a word that will not be revoked</u>: Before me every knee will bow; by me every tongue will swear.*
>
> *They will say of me, 'In the LORD alone are righteousness and strength.'" All who have raged against him will come to him and be put to shame.*
>
> —Isaiah 45:23-24 (emphasis added)

Our sin is nothing less than an attempt to elevate ourselves above God's holiness, to become *like* God. And there is only one possible response to this from the Judge of all—and that is infinite wrath. Any request for any other response could only come from one who did not understand, as I now do, the true nature of infinite holiness.

Almighty God's equally immeasurable wrath will hit them before any human thought or action or effort is even possible. They will get what they have blindly desired all of their lives, *freedom from God.* And their *hell* will be their knowledge that for all eternity they can never know He Who is their only completion. All are created such that only Jesus can be the full realization of all that they are meant to be. Jesus called all of us to Himself.

> *"But I, when I am lifted up from the earth, <u>will draw all men to myself</u>."*
>
> —John 12:32 (emphasis added)

In contrast, I now know only joy. This is the full joy of the knowledge that my salvation from God's just wrath had thankfully not relied upon *my* strength. It had been the sole responsibility of Jesus, fully God.

And with my face buried deep in the blood-soaked dirt at the foot of the cross of my Savior's sacrifice, I feel His touch. I feel the soft touch of my Savior's hand in my hand as my body is slowly lifted up. And I stand face to face *with Jesus*.

> *Then he placed his right hand on me and said: "Do not be afraid. I am the First and the Last. I am the Living One; I was dead, and behold I am alive for ever and ever! And I hold the keys of death and Hades."*
>
> —Revelation 1:17-18

I am now in the solitary presence of *the One* who is the very literal fulfillment of every thought, emotion, and desire that I experienced during the 62 years of my life. *Jesus*. Every sweet smell I ever breathed in was but a passing premonition of what I now experience. *Jesus*. Every beautiful sight my eyes ever beheld—especially the ones that took my breath away and filled me with a sense of something more to be beheld—were mere appetizers compared to the banquet feast now set before my eyes. *Jesus*.

> *Your eyes will see the king in his beauty...*
>
> —Isaiah 33:17

Every glorious song my ears have heard, every captivating refrain that rippled my earthly skin with goose bumps was but a brassy portent of the sound that fills my ears and vibrates every molecule of my being in the presence of my King. Every thundering finale of every event I have ever cherished, every moment of love for another person I have ever known, every tear and every laugh and every smile—they were all such shallow previews of the emotion that I now feel for my Redeemer.

Jesus.

The fullness of all that I now experience has been that ever-present shadow behind the momentary taste of the eternal reality that intermittently surfaced during my life. And best of all—indeed the very best of all—were the cavalry-to-the-rescue, last-minute-save, crescendo tears of joy that I experienced during my life every time God played out one of His incredible rescues. For God had written these rescue episodes in every one of our lives to give us a hint, a fleeting taste, of the fulfillment of our hearts desire that could only be found in His presence.

Indeed there was a reason that the episodes in my life that evoked the deepest emotional responses had all been *rescues*. For rescue is what Jesus is all about. All of those emotion-filled moments during my life gave me but a minute taste of the very majesty of this redemption meeting. The chest-deep sigh, the uncontrollable welling of tears, the shiver of knowing that there was so much more going on than I could see—they had all been the very real touch of God in my life. And now the distinct memories of these life events all melted into the most overwhelming-in-every-sense, stunningly magnificent feeling as all of my senses, heart, mind, and soul come into sharp focus on the very real presence of God.

And that face—the face of Jesus—the face that I had unknowingly sought with all of my heart for years.

> *My heart says of you, "Seek his face!" Your face, LORD, I will seek.*
> —(Psalm 27:8)

His face is now figuratively and literally mine to see. For now I stare into the eyes of God. And all is so new and so wonderful and so complete, yet somehow so familiar. *For I have seen this face before.* In fact, I have seen it a thousand times before. The visage that now fills my consciousness was mine to see throughout my life. For God had given me so many glimpses of it before. Its features, its likeness—subtle hints of it—had been present in every face of *every* person that I had interacted with every day of my life. It is literally as it had been stated:

> *"Then the King will say to those on his right, 'Come, you who are blessed by my Father; take your inheritance, the kingdom prepared for you since the creation of the world. For I was hungry and you gave me something to eat, I was thirsty and you gave me something to drink, I was a stranger and you invited me in, I needed clothes and you clothed me, I was sick and you looked after me, I was in prison and you came to visit me.' Then the righteous will answer him, 'Lord, when did we see you hungry and feed you, or thirsty and give you something to drink? When did we see you a stranger and invite you in, or needing clothes and clothe you? When did we see you sick or in prison and go to visit you?'*
>
> *"The King will reply, 'I tell you the truth, whatever you did for one of the least of these brothers of mine, you did for me.'"*
> —Matthew 25:34-40 (emphasis added)

In every face, I had figuratively—and now I realize, very literally—seen the face of my Redeemer. Oh, how this changes everything. Every face that I had been drawn to during my life, every face that had brought up unknown feelings and emotions, every face that made me smile, every face that evoked heartfelt compassion—they are all in the likeness of the face at which I now unabashedly stare.

I can't take my eyes off of Him. The emotion that overwhelms me now is nothing less than the culmination, the summation, of every time I looked into the eyes of the loves of my life—my wife, my children. For every time that I stared into the face of my beloved, I was staring into the face of my Beloved. The attraction is irresistible. Elements of it had been in every one of the faces to which I had been drawn, the faces that had elicited an uncontrollable smile every time I had seen them. Such is the face of my One and Only. Such is the face of Jesus.

And how I love to look at Him.

God. The very word had restrained my understanding of the infinitely immense—yet intensely personal—individual in whose presence I now stand. Jesus. How I now regret every casual reference to *God* that I made during my life. How could I have been so blind? Now that I stand in His Presence, the purity of the Light that pours forth from Him totally overwhelms me. I can no longer imagine how any being at any time could even think the word *God* without immediately falling to his face in worship. Reverence overwhelms me now. How I wish that I could take back every single unworthy thought of—let alone casual spoken reference to—*God.*

I can't take my eyes off of Him. *Jesus*! The True Light. The Lamb as He had been slain and yet at the same time the Lion of the Tribe of Judah. *Jesus*! My Savior. My Rock. My Redeemer. *Jesus*! The Water of Life and the Bread of Life. The Alpha and the Omega. The Beginning and the End. *Jesus.* The Word. The Logos. The very expression of the Living God. The Great I AM. The son of man and the only Son of God.

> *... he sees God's face and shouts for joy...*
>
> —Job 33:26

Jesus together simultaneously—separate but in unity—with the Father. And the vision of both is engulfed in the outpouring of the Spirit of the Living God, all not even fathomable during my life. This experience of God was not even approachable in the limitations of mind and heart that had defined my life. How telling of my naïveté—that I had often wondered how the cherubim, the *"highest"* of the created beings who *"day and night ... never stop saying: 'Holy, holy, holy is the Lord God Almighty, who was, and is, and is to come'" (Revelation 4:8)*, could be satisfied with an eternity of simply repeating those words. Now, in the presence of God, I know. For the very fact that their only desire is to do exactly that—to repeat the most holy of words of reverence to God for all eternity—is precisely what defines them as the highest of created beings. For only they fully comprehend that God is so totally not like them. He is not like any of the created beings. He is not the highest of beings for He could not even be classified as a *being* in the same sentence with any of the created. He is *set apart*. He is completely unlike any of them. He dwells in eternity. None of the properties of time and space and matter apply to Him in any respect. He is *holy* as it is truly and infinitely defined.

And here is Jesus, the rock-bottom valley of meekness and the highest mountain peak of strength. Fully God, He was yet willing to take on the skin of man for eternity. He is the very embodiment of perfect humility in all of human history— yet also the only awesome, awful-in-His-holiness, overpowering, breathtaking-beyond-all-comprehension, fearsome Force in the universe. Yet describing Him as such is demeaning, inadequate. Those words are so limiting to the very personal Presence that I now know. For the Presence before me is the only source of power—the only source of anything—in the universe for all eternity and beyond. He is truly the beginning. He is truly the end. He is the ultimate yearning and the perfect fulfillment of that yearning, the ultimate surrender and the ultimate victory.

And all is mine in the moment of my death.

Chapter 2

The Lamb

In the moment of my death, there is an immediate understanding, an immediate appreciation. I had sought exactly such pure truth in those rare moments during my life when my will and the will of the Holy Spirit had been coincident. But then my mind and heart and soul were simply incapable of encompassing the truth of the crucifixion.

It had not been just a man who had died on that hill 2000 years before. It had been the Son *of God*. And as the Son of God, He shares the very nature of God. The many attributes that God has allowed mankind to know of Him—His omnipotence, His love, His transcendence, His justice, His mercy, His compassion, His unchanging character, His righteousness, His Holiness, His perfection, His wisdom, His purity—all are now described completely only by the addition of the adjective *infinite*. What had that word *infinite* meant during my life? And what exactly did it mean that Jesus was the Son of God? Now I know that the answers to these two questions are encompassed in the pinnacle moment of the crucifixion.

Until this moment, when I finally rise to stand before my Savior and Redeemer, I could only imagine—no matter how much time I had spent meditating upon it— what the crucifixion of Jesus of Nazareth really meant. To stand in the presence of that which I had previously not been able to contemplate or experience, let alone fully understand, very literally overwhelms me. But it is exactly that knowledge that completes me, for now I know Jesus as He really is.

> *How great is the love the Father has lavished on us, that we should be called children of God! And that is what we are! The reason the world does not know us is that it did not know him.*
>
> *Dear friends, now we are children of God, and what we will be has not yet been made known. But we know that when he appears, we shall be like him, <u>for we shall see him as he is</u>.*
>
> —1John 3:1-2 (emphasis added)

Jesus. The Word. The *Logos*. Infinite perfection. Infinite purity. Infinite holiness. The word *infinite* had been undefinable during my life, especially in regard to the description of God's attributes. How could I have understood *infinite* then when nothing in my life could be described as such? But now I know it's meaning, it's true significance when applied as an adjective to those words that describe my King—and now it is the basis for all.

In this moment as I look into the face of my Redeemer, I know even more. In this moment I understand precisely what I deserve for my role as a singular definable point of intense rebellion against a righteous and holy God. I now fully comprehend what I had earned, and very much deserved, for the many times I blatantly and knowingly—and vehemently—defied my Creator and the very Object of my whole being.

And that horribly *just* payment is precisely what—in the very deepest depths of my soul where I have not often plumbed—is the most unimaginable of terrors: Infinite, perfect wrath.

Infinite wrath. I had never heard that word used to describe wrath. This just sweeps me away. I am very literally overwhelmed by the full and complete realization of what this means. The Lamb, who now stands before me in this moment of moments, had endured the Father's infinite wrath just for me. Although unimaginable then, in my transformed state I now know exactly what this means. I also know that Jesus made that trip up that hill with—somehow— only me on His mind. I know that Jesus had endured, for the first time and the only time in all eternity, that which had been exclusively reserved for those who chose by their own free will to be separated from God: perfect, total, infinite wrath.

> *Why, O LORD, do you reject me and hide your face from me? From my youth I have been afflicted and close to death; I have suffered your terrors and am in despair. Your wrath has swept over me; your terrors have destroyed me.*
>
> —Psalm 88:14-16

Words like staggering, heinous, and overwhelming are simply inadequate. Truly infinite wrath is not describable. Nonetheless, precisely that—the infinite wrath of the cross of Jesus—was mandatory for my salvation. God's judgment is simply not separable from His love, His justice totally inseparable from His mercy. In the consideration of sinful man, the only possible solution to the conundrum of the simultaneous existence of God's perfect justice and perfect mercy is the atoning death of God's only Son on the cross of Calvary. No *better* solution is possible, no other solution is possible: justice served—and yet mercy still extended to the unrighteous.

I know what every *believer* has to know. For I now face the stark reality of the intensely personal nature of my Savior's death on the cross of Calvary. I now know that the very image of my face had been on the mind of the King of kings as He took every step up that long winding road to Golgotha. I know that the thoughts of my Savior had been of me—Nathaniel—somehow for the entire time that He was on the cross. Not a fleeting *time-share* token moment shared with millions of other believers, but instead—somehow—of me alone for the entire time. Me alone—and yet somehow not alone.

Jesus had died for me. Jesus had endured the infinite wrath of the Father that was owed to me in payment for my rebellious sin against the very knowledge of God. From before time, Jesus had known of that moment in my sophomore year in college when I would take a blind step of faith toward the God of all creation. That moment had been all that was on His mind. For the joy that Jesus experienced was that He and I would spend eternity together because of the sacrifice before Him on the cross, and He had loved me intensely. He had loved me for all eternity and He had loved me on that cross as if I was the only one who would take that saving step of faith. That is the infinitely personal nature of that moment on Calvary. The reality of that knowledge is too much for me to bear. There is no more attempting to hide in anonymity among the huddled masses. This is face-to-face with the One who had borne for me the wrath of Almighty God.

I had not known what force had driven my face so completely and so quickly to the ground in that moment when I had first entered the presence of God. Had it been the powerful warrior cherubim? Was it merely the very fact of standing in the presence of perfect, complete holiness? Was it the now complete knowledge of the awesome, previously indescribable power found only in the presence of God? Or, and this overwhelms my mind, was it the knowledge of the unsounded, immeasurable depth of the debt that had been paid by my Savior's love for me? I am not sure; I know only that the Spirit of Jesus is in my heart and that there was only one possible response to the Presence I encountered immediately upon my death.

Chapter 3

My Body

As I now rise face-to-face with my Redeemer I become immediately and intensely aware of my body. The decayed human body that I had worn during my life is gone. I have a new body. It is clothed in white linen. My new body is one that I know in every detail, yet one that I have never seen before. My touch on every fingertip—yet at the same time over every inch of my new body—is overwhelmed by sensations that somehow *complete* everything that I had ever touched during my life. My nostrils are filled with the most pleasing of smells. My ears are filled and resonate with a single composition of so many beautiful sounds.

All of my senses are merged into a glorious unity of sensation. They blend together like the colors of a rainbow. Each is magnificent in its individual hue but finds completeness only as a component of a single brilliant entity. Each discrete sense is individually more magnificent (but that really is not an adequate description), each more complete in combination with the others. All of my sensorium is now complete in every definition of the word. This is the height and the width and the depth of the infinity that is found only in God.

At this moment all of my senses are flooded with the perception of wholeness, of fullness, of the infinite completeness of God. I feel as if I simply can't get enough of it. As I look beyond my Savior's eyes into the deep spaces of infinity, I see—all somehow instantaneously—every yearning, every desire, every longing, every thing or person or feeling that I had ever ached for in my whole life. A torrent of vivid memories of every beautiful sunset, every pretty girl's face, every anticipated vacation, every longed-for first date, every big business deal, every physical desire, every hunger, every thirst—memories of every thing I had ever longed for in deep anticipation of fulfillment—are all there simultaneously and instantaneously.

All that I had so longed for is fulfilled, completely and in formerly unknowable depth, in the person of Jesus Christ.

> Then Jesus declared, "I am the bread of life. He who comes to me will never go hungry, and he who believes in me will never be thirsty."

—John 6:35

He is the fulfillment, the completion, the magnification of every thing that I had ever sought during my life. These longings during my life had been so many daily small tastes of the fulfillment, of the *completion*, for which I was created.

> *Now this is eternal life: that they may know you, the only true God, and Jesus Christ, whom you have sent.*
> —John 17:3

For the Creator had created the created for the Creator, purely and exclusively.

During my life the realization of these longings, these cravings, had always been incomplete. It had, like the bloom of a flower, been transient and always faded away. The greatest vacation had always ended. The joy of the fame from closing the big business deal had always diminished. That incomparable infatuation with the pretty face had always grown fainter. The physical desire had always withered away. The hunger and the thirst had always returned.

But not now.

Now nothing fades. Everything is complete. The satiation of each and every desire by the Person of Jesus Christ is almost overwhelming. Instead of fading, the feelings of satisfaction only intensify.

> *Jesus answered, "Everyone who drinks this water will be thirsty again, but whoever drinks the water I give him will never thirst. Indeed, the water I give him will become in him a spring of water welling up to eternal life."*
> —John 4:13-14

Now, inherent in the very nature of this perfect fulfillment of every deep desire is *even more desire*! Not only is there even more desire, but also the *capacity* for even more fulfillment—for more of Him. With every bit of the ever-expanding capacity of my being to do so, I reflexively, automatically, impulsively lunge toward my God with all of my strength. I lunge with all of the strength of my entire mind, soul, and heart. My deep desire to know God with every sense—that which I had only tasted intermittently and transiently during my life—is completely fulfilled. Yet I instantaneously long for more and that also is immediately fulfilled. A continuous flow of desire is somehow met by a continuous flow of satisfaction from the truly *infinite* abundance that is God. Breathtaking tumultuous joy overwhelms me, yet it occurs simultaneously with contentment and rest. All continues to redefine my understanding of the word *infinite* and its application to God and eternity. For I, Nathaniel, the *finite* created being, now know the endless exhilarating satisfaction found in the infinite God. All that I was created for is mine for eternity.

> *One thing I ask of the LORD, this is what I seek: that I may dwell in the house of the LORD all the days of my life, to gaze upon the beauty of the LORD and to seek him in his temple.*
>
> *—Psalm 27:4*

Chapter 4

The Angel Gabriel

My new body enjoys the infinite capacity to breathe in every sensation that emanates from the One who stands before me. I can't take my eyes off Him. This is Jesus—my Everything, my Beginning and my End. I now exist totally in a state of simultaneous flooding of the need for more of Him and the instantaneous fulfillment of that very need. There is always more desire and yet always more simultaneous fulfillment. There is simply no thought of taking my eyes off Him. I am complete in Him. There is no need, there is no desire, there is nothing outside of Him. I cannot smell anything else, I cannot hear anything else, I cannot feel anything else, I cannot see anything else...*and yet I can.*

I can sense *others* around me. I can sense them without taking my eyes and the attention of every hyper-excited sense of my body off my King and Redeemer. Somehow, that which was impossible during my life is now not only possible, it is absolute in the expanded dimensions of eternity: the perpetual complete knowledge and praise of the Living God *while simultaneously thinking and interacting with the other persons and the environment around me.*

> *They rejoice in your name <u>all</u> day long.*
>
> —Psalm 89:16 (emphasis added)

> *Blessed are those who dwell in your house; they are <u>ever</u> praising you.*
>
> —Psalm 84:4 (emphasis added)

That which I had sought with all my might and prayer during my life—the uninterrupted knowledge of the most holy God—is now completely and perfectly and infinitely mine. And I know the will of God. I know exactly what, when, and how I am to proceed on the adventure before me.

The adventure? Oh yes, there is the anticipation of even more. Yet at all times I stand and feel and experience all in the presence of Jesus—continually! The continuity with Jesus is the foundation of the perfect, majestic fulfillment of the mind and body that I only thought I knew during my life. This is an experience never imagined outside of the presence of God. All is woven together. Everything occurs simultaneously and together, yet everything seems separate, delightfully distinct, and apart in time.

The words of the angel Gabriel to Zechariah flash immediately into my consciousness. Not a paraphrase, but the exact Aramaic words *and* a complete understanding of them, for Jesus illuminates them for me now: *"... I stand in the presence of God"* (Luke 1:19). Not *"I have stood in the presence of God."* Not *"I will stand in the presence of God."* Not *"I have just come from standing in the presence of God."* No. The words are very clear. *"I stand in the presence of God. Now, as I talk to you, at this very instant, I see Him and know Him and feel Him and understand His will—I stand in the presence of God."*

It is all clear now. These words, which I had pondered as curious and peculiar as I read them during my life, are now so obvious and so clear in their meaning. This is the true *reality* that had been behind the façade that the world had declared real during my lifetime.

> *So we fix our eyes not on what is seen, but on what is unseen. For what is seen is temporary, but what is unseen is eternal.*
> —2Corinthians 4:18

The words of Jesus recorded in the Gospel of Matthew also ring ever so delightfully in my ears now:

> *"See that you do not look down on one of these little ones. For I tell you that their angels in heaven always see the face of my Father in heaven."*
> —Matthew 18:10 (emphasis added)

In these words, *"their angels in heaven always see the face of my Father in heaven,"* had been a tiny taste, another hint of eternity. Jesus had tried to tell me that the angels stand simultaneously in heaven in the presence of God—staring continually into His face—all the while that they stand guard over *"these little ones."* Now I know what He was talking about. Now I know that there is no way that any sentient created being can look away from the face of Almighty God once they have laid eyes on Him. But now, in the expanded dimensions of my eternity, I don't have to look away. My mind and the senses of my body are no longer limited to just four dimensions. I am in direct, palpable contact with, and capable of full physical interaction with, the people and environment around me, while simultaneously—through six additional dimensions—charging headlong with all of my might into the knowledge of the Most Holy.

> *From birth I have relied on you; you brought me forth from my mother's womb. I will <u>ever</u> praise you. My mouth is filled with your praise, declaring your splendor <u>all</u> day long.*
> —Psalm 71:6,8 (emphasis added)

Chapter 5

The Word of God to Man

The written Word of God, every stroke of God's perfect pen, is all here. Nothing is missing and all of the Word is illuminated in the fullness of the infinite knowledge of its Author. But God is more than its Author. The written Word is the very expression of Him. It is the *Logos*. Jesus is the full manifestation of God to mankind—and the written Word is all about Him. Together, they are the Word, the *Logos*, the very expression of God to man. Jesus is the interface between the created and the Uncreated—and the written Word tells us how. Jesus is the bridge that crosses the infinite gap between that which cannot be connected and that which cannot exist without connection—and the written Word illuminates His path. Jesus is the interface between the unconnectable—and the written Word explains the unexplainable.

It is exactly as I had suspected during my life. The written Word of God had in fact been so perfectly complete there before me. As the infinitely perfect expression of God, it can't be anything but perfectly complete. For it is the whole expression of Him, *whole* in every expression of the word. God is infinite, and the written Word is mysteriously, gloriously infinite in its perfect characterization of the Living God. During my life I had only scratched the surface of the unknowable depth of everything that the Word so loudly proclaimed before me. It is utterly magnificent in its infinite depth. Now I know why each and every time that I had read it during my life, it had somehow spoken differently, in some new and wonderful way, to the deep places of my heart.

But now the written Word is all here. It explains, expands, and illuminates everything. It is perfectly, permanently, and blazingly inscribed on the awareness that is my mind. Every word is here and every word has infinity behind it. Every space between every word is filled with infinite expression. Nothing is missing. Each paragraph transcends the depths of my vision. The Word is truly infinitely deep, just like its Author, just like the One that it fully reveals. It is infinitely pure and perfect and complete, just as I had somehow known it would be. It is the very expression of the infinite God. It is mine to know and explore and delight in for all eternity

A previously inconceivable knowledge fills my mind. Somehow I have immediate, complete knowledge and simultaneous recall of every second of my entire life: the good times, when I had made the right choices that glorified my Savior; and the bad times, when I chose the world over my Redeemer and held all that now fulfills me in rebellious, unholy contempt. But now even these also glorify God since the full display of His perfect mercy is illuminated for all that it truly is in the depth of my moral bankruptcy. The written Word is there in the midst of every second of my life. It is wrapped in and out of every crevice of every event of every day of my life. My life had been so complete in its illustration of everything that is written there. God had made my life experience, as He had with every other human life, complete in every respect, complete in its illumination of the Word.

For now I know that every day of my life had been orchestrated by the indescribable magnificence that is God. His purpose was purely and pointedly to bring me to an understanding and experience of the very nature of God. For God had known, before time began, of my every response to every test that He would set before me. Every battle, every test, every situation, every challenge, every person, every relationship that I had always believed to be a result of mere random happenstance, had *all* been planned. Every one. Each and every daily event or meeting had been exactly and perfectly orchestrated by the all-knowing, all wise, and all good master artistry of the Living God. All had been planned and all had been necessary to get me precisely where God wanted me to go.

For with His foreknowledge of that moment when I accepted the salvation found in my Redeemer's shed blood, God had orchestrated perfection into my life. It was God's perfection, God's infinite wisdom aimed at taking me exactly and perfectly to the righteousness that God had called me to—nothing less than to be molded into the very likeness of Jesus.

Each and every event or test or person that I had encountered, every single moment of my life was an expression of the perfection of God. There was no random happenstance. In every case, each interaction was in fact the perfect event at the perfect time necessary to move me one step closer to God's perfect end. All of those events that I had labeled as "good luck," and all of those events that I had railed angrily against as just "bad luck," are all defined as *good* in God's infinitely perfect eternal perspective. By the very definition of God's perfection there could not have been a better way. There could not have even been *another* way. There was only one way and that was, within the confines of and full pre-knowledge of my free-will choices, exactly the way it had occurred.

> *"Do not tremble, do not be afraid.* <u>*Did I not proclaim this and foretell it long ago*</u>*? You are my witnesses. Is there any God besides me? No, there is no other Rock; I know not one."*
> —Isaiah 44:8 (emphasis added)

For God had, before time began, known my free-will response to every event. God had carefully orchestrated the subsequent events in response to the closely guarded free will of His beloved Nathaniel. No matter what I chose to do, whether right or wrong, God always had another event, another challenge, another encounter that took me closer and closer to a full knowledge of Him.

> *"Have you not heard? Long ago I ordained it. In days of old I* <u>*planned*</u> *it; now I have* <u>*brought it to pass*</u>*…"*
> —Isaiah 37:26 (emphasis added)

> *Before a word is on my tongue you know it completely, O LORD.* <u>*You hem me in*</u>*—*<u>*behind and before*</u>*; you have laid your hand upon me.*
> —Psalm 139:4-5 (emphasis added)

The gift of free will and freedom of choice always carefully and uncompromisingly guarded—yet I, Nathaniel, *called* and *justified* perfectly.

> *My purpose will stand, and I will do all that I please.*
> —Isaiah 46:10

> *What I have said, that will I bring about; what I have planned, that will I do.*
> —Isaiah 46:11

This magnificent plan for my life was enabled and empowered by God's foreknowledge, before time began, of my freewill choice of Him. Each individual trial or encounter or event, was therefore, the product of all three—my previous choices, God's knowledge of my future choices, and God's desired endpoint.

> *All the days ordained for me were written in your book before one of them came to be.*
> —Psalm 139:16

And it really was exactly as I had feared that it might be when I had railed angrily against God during the most difficult chapters of my life. Now I know that there had, in fact, simply never been a justification for my questioning of God's goodness or His faithful and loving presence in my life—even during those troublesome times of testing.

I know that every life is as complete as mine, every life perfect in its artistry and knowledge. Every life is a perfect manifestation of that which is *the Word* of the awesome God.

Chapter 6

The Reward

The more I now move toward God, the more I marvel at the resulting conspicuous change in myself. The Word of God had foretold it well. All is now perfection in the frustration of the so-called *wisdom* of the world. For now, the more I move toward God, the more independent I become. I recognize now that this had also been true during my life. The more I focus on God and the more I seek *His* will, the more the uniqueness of my personality becomes manifest. The more my mind and soul and heart turn toward and focus upon the One and Only, the more that I become aware of in my surroundings. The more I strive to interact with God, the more enabled I become to interact with all that is around me. The more I surrender to the Lamb, the more empowered I become. The more I allow myself to be defeated by this awesome power, the more victorious I feel. Complete surrender. Complete victory. Complete victory in complete surrender—exactly as Jesus had perfectly modeled on the cross. There is no rebellion in my heart now. The rebellion has finally ended.

This is the reward, the reward of which the prophets and apostles had so often spoken. My reward is the knowledge of the Person of Jesus Christ. I simply can't get enough of it. This is what my heart had been created for, nothing less, and there could be nothing more. I gulp it all in, huge voluminous drafts from the keg of God's glory. This is my reward now, the full knowledge of the complete manifestation of God. It is as full, that is, as a created being can know. For none, except the three Persons of the Trinity, can truly know the infinite expanse of God. Exploring this infinity is the eternity of the redeemed—forever discovering the infinite Godhead, and being nourished and satisfied by the very knowledge of the Only Holy. The simultaneous anticipation and satiation of that desire is now the joy of my heart and it is infinite.

The more I gave myself to God during my life, the more I grew in my knowledge of the Holy One. The more I chose God over non-God, the more I came to know the presence and touch and face of the Only One. In exactly this is the promised reward, more even than I could have ever imagined. Indeed, all that I had done in the will of God is immediately and palpably in my consciousness now. It now forms the basis of my knowledge of my Savior. *It* is the reward. *It* is the crown. *It* is the end. My earthly deeds, based on my faith and belief, were but the means to that end. They are unmistakable evidence of the very merciful grace of God. It is all so magnificently clear to me now.

With all of this has come the simultaneous awareness of people all around me. I see the vast body of the redeemed, of which I am a part. We are the unified body of Christ, His bride. We are all adorned in the jewels of God's grace and dressed eternally in linen washed white by the blood of the Lamb. *One* bonded wholly to *the One*. Yet, at the same time, each and every one of us is a distinct individual. All of us are moving with a singular purpose, yet each is moving within a simultaneously unique facet of that purpose. All are moving as individuals performing their tasks—which no one else in all of the body could do as well and as completely—yet all moving to fulfill the unified, singular will of the Lord of lords and the King of kings.

All of us move deliberately now toward our assigned tasks. I speak with those around me, joyfully, simultaneously, all in the knowledge and continual presence of Jesus. There is no need to renew old acquaintances. I know these wonderful people. And they know me. They know the good and the bad about my life and I know the same about theirs. We know all of the details of each others' lives, and none of it matters except where it had brought glory to the Name above all names. For our focus now is not on ourselves. It is on each other. And, by being on each other, it is on him. It is on Him, and—somehow—on Him alone. His presence overwhelms every earthly desire. His continual presence fills every void. There is only Him. At the same time there is everything and everyone else...yet there is only Him.

Each of us knows every part of each other's lives. There is nothing to be ashamed of, for there is only Him. All of us had sinned. Each of us had committed every sin described in the written Word of God. All were equally bad. And among these warriors gathered here in His name, all are equally forgiven. Each of us says, *"I sinned, and perverted what was right, but I did not get what I deserved. He redeemed my soul from going down to the pit, and I will live to enjoy the light"* *(Job 33:27-28)*. Each of us knows Jesus in a very special way, a way that is peculiar to our individual lives and the personalities with which God had gifted each of us. Each is peculiar in our individual sin and in our individual triumphs. Each is so similar in so many ways and yet so unique in our individual knowledge of the Living God.

I know that my extraordinary and very special knowledge of Jesus, different from that of any other person, is based almost entirely upon the special ways that I, by God's grace, had managed to honor God during my life. This knowledge is the *white stone* that had been promised.

> *He who has an ear, let him hear what the Spirit says to the churches. To him who overcomes, I will give some of the hidden manna. <u>I will also give him a white stone with a new name written on it, known only to him who receives it</u>.*
>
> —Revelation 2:17 (emphasis added)

On this knowledge, this stone, is written a very special name. Not a name like *Nathaniel*. But an identity with the Living God and with His Son that is totally and wholly and incredibly personal and unique to me. Only They know this special identity. This unique identity is the name that has been etched on the white stone by the finger of God—since the beginning of time.

For every time during my life that I chose God over the overwhelming lure of Satan and the world and my flesh, God had been glorified. The heavenly host had rejoiced. Jesus remembers every episode, every detail of every episode. Even the tiniest of decisions for Jesus are now magnified in their revelation and amplified in their praise of the Living God. Now they are fully known by all. Each experience had been a test. They were tests, devised in the vast unfathomable mind of the Living God before time began, tests intended to search every heart.

> *"And you, my son Solomon, acknowledge the God of your father, and serve him with wholehearted devotion and with a willing mind, <u>for the LORD searches every heart and understands every motive behind the thoughts</u>. If you seek him, he will be found by you; but if you forsake him, he will reject you forever."*
>
> —1Chronicles 28:9 (emphasis added)

They were tests to reveal what was truly in our hearts. They were no revelation to God. He already knew the condition of our hearts. They were instead intended *for us*.

> *I also thought, "As for men, God tests them so that they may see that they are like the animals."*
>
> —Ecclesiastes 3:18

They were tests to help us know the very depths of our hearts. For a full knowledge of God can only come after a complete knowledge of the utter bankruptcy of our hearts and our complete impotence against the will of our rebellious natures. These tests occurred that we might know our hearts, but also to make us declare to ourselves and before the entire creation, whether we were for God or for the world. All must declare, one way or the other.

They were tests designed by our Creator to exercise that which He valued most in each one of us, that special gift that He had given us—the freedom to choose between God and non-God. Each test was designed to challenge the individual and his use of that gift. Two choices were always offered. It was always a choice between God and the world; God's way or the world's way, God or non-God, God or self, good or evil. So many chances to bring glory to God—and so many missed for all eternity.

Ah, but by the grace of God there were those occasional home runs, the purely selfless choices, the complete surrender, the choice of Jesus. How much our Savior values our free choice of Him. For in every free choice of the knowledge of God is the reminder of all that the Father has had to endure, the reminder of so many bad choices and so many children lost. This is the sorrow and grief of Almighty God, all endured just to make this free choice of God possible. To be able to choose God, one also had to be able to not choose God. Now I share these experiences of the choice of God, and the glory they imparted to the Father, continually with Jesus—and for all eternity. Those around me cheer for me, and I cheer for them, all simultaneously while we are moving toward our assigned tasks.

Chapter 7

The Deep

Through this entire cascade of mental and physical activity I desire to experience even more of *the One* who always stands before me—Jesus. I thought that I had known Him during my life. Now, every desire of my body, mind, and heart is unified in the singular purpose of moving farther into the knowledge and presence of Jesus. I want to move closer to the One who is now so perfectly close.

> *I have given them the glory that you gave me, that they may be one as we are one: I in them and you in me. May they be brought to complete unity to let the world know that you sent me and have loved them even as you have loved me.*
>
> —John 17:22-23

I want even more of *the One* whose presence is already wholly and perfectly manifest—and yet always offers even more. As every fibre of my being strives to move directly into this knowledge, to be entirely engulfed by this experience of Him, still every feeling is of contentment. Somehow, the overwhelming feeling of an all-consuming, heart-felt desire for the only source of joy, coexists simultaneously with its immediate realization—total joy in the knowledge and presence of Him who I desire. My desire is frenetic, yet my joy is complete and somehow absolute.

It is all so overwhelming. Yet in the midst of it all, I know that I want still more—infinitely more—and this desire moves me closer and further into the knowledge of the Only Holy. Yet again, my movement into the knowledge and presence of Jesus only accelerates my desire to know and experience more of Him. With this accelerating desire comes the simultaneous, extraordinary joy of anticipation. I know my desire will be—is being—met. I am like a child on Christmas morning or a lover in anticipation of a first kiss. I am overwhelmed by a feeling that was unknown during my life—actually, an unimaginable feeling during my life—of an ever-accelerating velocity of desire. Not just increasing desire, but a rapidly increasing increase of that desire.

This is the *deep*. It is like being shot out of a cannon directly into the love of Jesus, which is the only satisfaction, the only completion, the only fulfillment of all that I am. It is overwhelming, infinite desire—and complete realization of that desire. It is a state of perpetual contentment. It is *rest*—in a state of continual exhilaration. Yet still it is rest. This is the deep.

The deep can only be described in terms that were so unfamiliar to me during my life. It is a continually increasing velocity. It is a continually increasing velocity in the desire, and simultaneous fulfillment of that desire, for the knowledge and experience and presence of God. It is the continual feeling that there is more to be had, something attainable just beyond where I am—and I must have it. As my desire for more continually accelerates, I realize that my desire for Jesus is infinite—infinite, as He is infinite. The anticipation of fulfillment itself is pure joy. And most emphatically, of even more importance, I know that the simultaneous ability of God to fulfill that desire, to fill me with the knowledge and understanding of the person of God, is also infinite. *Infinite*. The infinite God. I had often wondered what that really meant during my life. Now it is my very existence.

In the midst of all this, there is rest. There is more mental and physical activity than I experienced on the busiest day in my life and yet somehow there is no fatigue. My continual effort toward God is strenuous, far more strenuous than anything that I had known during my lifetime, yet I do not tire and I am content. Exhilarated rest. What? What a strange combination of words that would have been before I encountered the deep. Intense, irresistible, unquenchable desire exists simultaneously with contentment. It is a condition that had simply not existed in the untransformed state.

The cycle is so rapidly repeating—desire, joyous anticipation of fulfillment of that desire, joy in its actual fulfillment, still more desire, more joyous anticipation of fulfillment, more joy in its actual fulfillment—that it whirls phenomenally into a single, all-encompassing feeling of eternal infinite joy in the knowledge of the infinite God. This is the deep.

Equally perplexing is the fact that I am still very much Nathaniel Hawkens. I, Nathaniel, am not *lost* in my God as Satan had scorned and the nations had feared—to their eternal loss. Quite to the contrary. Not only am I the Nathaniel Hawkens that I knew during my life, but I am also the very complete fulfillment of all that was Nathaniel Hawkens. I am everything that I had been every minute of my life—all at once. Despite my movement in the body of the redeemed, and despite my single-minded, wholehearted craving and acceleration toward the knowledge of God, I am more of an individual than I had ever been during my life. My differences from all of those around me seem accentuated, heightened like my senses, and stark in the glorious uniqueness that they impart to me in the presence of all.

My distinctness from the others is simultaneously recognized and celebrated by those around me. It is celebrated in the unity of the body to which I now gloriously belong. I also celebrate the unique qualities of the individuals in that body. For their distinct, unique attributes are also held by no one else. That which had served to divide in the world now unites, as we all celebrate our individually incomparable reflections of the infinite facets of God. Gone is the jealousy, the envy, and the self. I know all of the redeemed as I had never known them during my life. Somehow I am completely dependent upon every one of them, yet simultaneously I am completely independent. How wrong the world's wisdom had been regarding the love and knowledge of God.

They who were of the world had been so vociferous in their warnings of the threatened loss of their coveted individuality. All would be lost if one submitted to the laws and decrees of this God of the Bible. There would be no individuality, just a blending of all into a robotic quagmire. They had hoarded that which had been a gift to them from the very Person they now scorned. But God had fooled the wise. In the futility of their own *wisdom* was the fulfillment of the promise of God.

> *"This is what the* LORD *says—your Redeemer, who formed you in the womb: I am the* LORD*, who has made all things, who alone stretched out the heavens, who spread out the earth by myself, who <u>foils the signs of false prophets and makes fools of diviners, who overthrows the learning of the wise and turns it into nonsense</u>..."*
> —Isaiah 44:24-25 (emphasis added)

I celebrated the wisdom of God with those around me. In submitting to God's decrees we had found true freedom, while those who gave into the ever-promising lies of the world had blended into an amorphic, homogeneous mass of trapped humanity, hopelessly fettered by the blindness of their sin. Everything that the world had tried to hide from me is not just true; it is exactly and totally true. I simply cannot take my eyes off the Lamb who had been slain.

However, as it is written: "No eye has seen, no ear has heard, no mind has conceived what God has prepared for those who love him"—but God has revealed it to us by his Spirit. The Spirit searches all things, even the deep things of God.

—1 Corinthians 2:9-10 (emphasis added)

Chapter 8

The Others

I have an eerie awareness of *others*. It is an awareness of those who had chosen poorly, of those who had repeatedly turned from the knowledge of God that He, in His loving grace, had continually poured over their very existence, over their every day. They had turned away—first subtly, then forcefully, then in an accelerating crescendo as God zealously tried to convince them of His goodness and love.

But they, in their love of themselves and of the world, had repeatedly turned from *the One* who loved and sought them. And as they had repetitively turned away, in little decisions to begin with, their blindness had grown. With each choice of non-God over God, the haze over their minds' eyes had gradually thickened.

> *They know nothing, they understand nothing; their eyes are plastered over so they cannot see, and their minds closed so they cannot understand.*
>
> —Isaiah 44:18

Even the obvious warnings became obscure as they chose the lusts of their bodies over the knowledge of the holy. When repeatedly faced with the only decision that really mattered among a million life decisions—the decision that all of those other decisions pointed toward—they had bought fully into the lies of Satan and the world. This is a decision that every person must face. This is a decision that must be made. Although the world tries to blur the edges and add to the confusion about it, the question is straightforward and clear:

"Who, exactly, is this Jesus of Nazareth?"

One's whole life—and one's whole eternity—hinges on the answer to this question. For if one believes that Jesus truly is exactly who He says He is—the only Son of the only God—then life-changing realization necessarily follows. For if He is the Son of God, then all that He said *is* true. His death *was* for the sins of all mankind and, most specifically and personally, for the individual making *the decision.* And, most critically, if He is the Son of God, then He *is* precisely that which He claimed to be: the *only* way to the Father and to eternal life.

Belief in the Name of Jesus changes everything. For if one truly believes, every thought, every word, every action from that moment forward must be tendered in the currency of God and His Holy Word. Although our vision may be blurred in the thick of the decision, this question really has only two possible answers and they are polar opposites—180 degrees in opposition to each other. The choice is black and white, and every person's answer must be cut and dry. You are either for Jesus or you are against Him. There is no hedging on this issue. God will not allow it. Every man and every woman must make a choice. To not decide—to hedge, to be *"lukewarm—neither hot nor cold" (Revelation 3:16)*—is no dodge. To not decide is to clearly and emphatically decide *against* Jesus.

Some of those who I sense around me now had simply said "No" and turned most definitely and most defiantly toward the course of the rest of their lives. Others had avoided the decision all of their lives. They had deluded themselves. This is the only decision that is mandatory for all men and women. Yes, it was the decision of decisions, and these had chosen poorly.

> *They have chosen their own ways, and their souls delight in their abominations; so I also will choose harsh treatment for them and will bring upon them what they dread. For when I called, no one answered, when I spoke, no one listened. They did evil in my sight and chose what displeases me.*
>
> —Isaiah 66:3-4 (emphasis added)

They had refused to repent. They had refused to surrender their hearts and their wills to Jesus, to the only One who offered them the hope of redemption. Theirs is eternal regret and, strangely, eternal anger.

> *Distress and anguish fill him with terror; they overwhelm him, like a king poised to attack, because he shakes his fist at God and vaunts himself against the Almighty, defiantly charging against him with a thick, strong shield.*
>
> —Job 15:24-26 (emphasis added)

Their lives had, for the most part, been the exact opposite of those who now surround me in the body of the redeemed and who, with me, celebrate the knowledge of God. For my brothers and sisters in Christ had lived for the words that fill my mind now:

> *This is the one I esteem: he who is humble and contrite in spirit, and trembles at my word.*
>
> —Isaiah 66:2

I had known many of those who now, forever separated, rage against God. Some I had loved. With some I had struggled. But now the Living Word, ever before me, reminds me that the *written* Word had spoken directly to all mankind of how they would be viewed now:

> *"And they will go out and look upon the dead bodies of those who rebelled against me; their worm will not die, nor will their fire be quenched, and they will be loathsome to all mankind."*
>
> —Isaiah 66:24 (emphasis added)

In their blindness they had hoped that in eternity they would "just be left alone." During their lives they thought that they had hidden in the anonymity of the masses. "Why can't I just continue to hide? I do just fine by myself. Why can't I just be left alone—forever?"

> *Yet they say to God, 'Leave us alone! We have no desire to know your ways.*
>
> —Job 21:14 (emphasis added)

> *At that time I will search Jerusalem with lamps and punish those who are complacent, who are like wine left on its dregs, who think, 'The LORD will do nothing, either good or bad.'*
>
> —Zephaniah 1:12 (emphasis added)

They had tried to make it anything but personal. But it is only and exactly and totally personal—the cross had made it that way. All that they dreaded might be true—is perfectly and obviously true. They did not need God then, and they rationalized that they would not need Him in eternity. They had all been offered the free gift; for God had given each of them a thousand chances to simply say, "yes." They only had to say it once and they would have, by His power only, been able to turn. But they had all repeatedly chosen to go it alone. And God had granted them completely, exclusively, exactly that which they had chosen.

That choice now defines the very boundaries of hell. They, as creatures created by God to know Him fully for eternity, rage now in the full knowledge of what it means to have no hope of ever being joined to that which they had been created to join. That is exactly and precisely what makes hell, hell.

For all can see that wise men die; the foolish and the senseless alike perish and leave their wealth to others. Their tombs will remain their houses forever, their dwellings for endless generations, though they had named lands after themselves. But man, despite his riches, does not endure; he is like the beasts that perish. This is the fate of those who trust in themselves, and of their followers, who approve their sayings. Selah

Like sheep they are destined for the grave, and death will feed on them. The upright will rule over them in the morning; their forms will decay in the grave, far from their princely mansions. But God will redeem my life from the grave; he will surely take me to himself. Selah

Do not be overawed when a man grows rich, when the splendor of his house increases; for he will take nothing with him when he dies, his splendor will not descend with him. Though while he lived he counted himself blessed—and men praise you when you prosper—he will join the generation of his fathers, who will never see the light [of life]. A man who has riches without understanding is like the beasts that perish.

—Psalm 49:10-20

There had been hints all through their lives of what would await them if they chose to refuse the free gift of salvation. And now they know the completion of, the fullest expression of the hints of emptiness and terror that He had shown them during their lives. Now they know only the deepest void of emptiness and the infinite fullness of terror.

He lies down wealthy, but will do so no more; when he opens his eyes, all is gone. Terrors overtake him like a flood; a tempest snatches him away in the night. The east wind carries him off, and he is gone; it sweeps him out of his place. It hurls itself against him without mercy as he flees headlong from its power.

—Job 27:19-22

They know only terror, while I know only joy. My joy is, in its entirety, found in the knowledge that He, whom I had been created to join and enjoy for eternity, could now never be separated from me—and this for all eternity.

> *My servants will sing out of the joy of their hearts, but you will cry out*
> *from anguish of heart and wail in brokenness of spirit.*

—Isaiah 65:14

Chapter 9

The Body of Christ

My relationship with all of those around me in eternity is a delightful surprise. There are so many wonderful individuals. Some I had known during my lifetime, most I had not. But—somehow—now I know them all. For now I interact with each of them while simultaneously in the presence of the Living God. Now Jesus speaks simultaneously to me about every person that I find myself engaging, a coincident ongoing conversation with me about that person. I delight in the extraordinary depth of the expression of His love for each of them. He continually praises each person's qualities. He sings songs of praise over them. He tells tales of valor. He recounts their every great chronicle of adventure and love. There is a continual, excited exchange about the pure joy that He finds in each of them. Each is a conversation that—and this is most important—means that I see them as Jesus sees them. Even in the overwhelming presence of the Almighty—*exactly* in the overwhelming presence of the Almighty—I retain the capacity to be absolutely captivated by each of them, just as Jesus is.

How Jesus loves them, and how I love them. Any self-imposed impediments to loving them during my life are now completely gone. For now I see them only through the loving eyes of their Redeemer and King. Each is of infinite worth to me because Jesus has declared them so. No longer does the cloud of my self-interest blur my vision of them. Any remaining self interest—and I think there really is none now—has been completely overcome by my overwhelming interest in Jesus. And through His eyes, I see them as they really are. They are magnificent! Each one is magnificent in his or her own very special way. No longer are they a threat or a competitor or a rival or an obstruction or a frustration or a cause for anxiety. Nor do they wear any of the other labels that the world had given them during my life. Now, my focus is no longer on the world around me, or on myself. It is on Jesus. I now see them, therefore, as Jesus has always seen them. I love them as Jesus has always loved them.

It is the same for them. Jesus simultaneously, continually praises me in His conversation with the person to whom I am speaking.

I now realize that this very same capacity to so deeply love those around me had also been there during my life. And yet my closed mind, hardened heart, and spiritual blindness had prevented me from entering into the full enjoyment of that capability. I had repeatedly experienced glimmers of this magnificent interaction in the body of Christ. There were times when I had stepped toward God and felt the presence of God so tangibly in my life. Those were times when I, by God's grace and mercy and presence in my heart, had been able to push my schemes, plots, fears, and presumptions aside, to allow my Savior's unconditional love to come forward. Those were unique and most holy times when I had then seen those around me through the compassion, forgiveness, mercy, and love that is the very essence of my Savior, Jesus. I had loved them then nearly as intensely as I do now. It is so easy—so humanly natural—to treat others perfectly when the lies of the world are stripped away by the presence of God. Now I see them perfectly, truthfully, for whom they truly are—magnificent people made faithfully in the likeness of the Living God. It truly is all about God. And yet, so often during my life I had made it all about myself.

How I wish that I had gone to my Savior Jesus before every interaction with every person that I had met during my life. For if I could have just seen them through His eyes, through His holy and eternal perspective, how much easier it would have been to show them compassion, to forgive and forget their every offense, to show them mercy in all situations, and to love them unconditionally as Jesus does. But my fears had triumphed so many times. I had not gone to my Savior. I had not loved.

Now I look back from eternity upon those many episodes when my blindness toward the people that God had brought into my life had left me so out of control—and I had hated them. Now I can see what periods of total blindness these had been. From my perspective in eternity now, where my eyes are permanently and undeniably fixed on Jesus, these episodes are utter darkness. Now it is so readily clear that the very presence of hatred had, every single time, been a wildly waving red flag that signaled a train gone uncontrollably off track, a flag that signaled a heart that was so focused on itself that it was incapable of forgiving.

For now, in the light that is Jesus, in the stark reality of the forgiveness that I have been granted when I so poignantly deserved none, it is so easy to forgive all. There simply is no other possible option. For now, in the presence of God, I know that the hatred had risen during my life from an unforgiving and fearful heart. Just like now, there had been no reason not to forgive and forget their offenses then. I simply have no excuse for these episodes. There had been no reason to act out of fear then, because then, just like now, there had been no reason to fear. In those dark life moments I am humbled and bankrupt. For true faith in Jesus had demanded the demonstration of the trust that He would do exactly what He said He would do—that He would always be there for me, that there was nothing to fear, that there was every reason to forgive. Instead, I had chosen to fear and in my fear there could be no forgiveness.

I regret every one of those episodes from the depths of my heart. Perhaps *regret* is not the right word for it, because the forgiveness bought by the death of my Savior on the cross of Calvary is complete in every manner. Still, in my eternity there is the remembrance of these special episodes where the blood of the Messiah's sacrifice ran especially red in my life. For I now know that in these interactions, these everyday interactions with the people that the Father had steered into my life, was where I had met my Redeemer…just as I know Him now. From every face—from every set of eyes—my Jesus had been looking back at me, just as He does now.

Chapter 10

The Wedding Feast

> *"The kingdom of heaven is like a king who prepared a wedding banquet for his son."*
>
> —Matthew 22:2

It is almost as I had imagined during my lifetime. Before me now is a great banquet table. It sits in a great banquet hall that is not a hall at all. The walls of this magnificent venue are majestic mountains. Their green slopes contrast against the bright blue sky and fluffy white clouds. The beauty takes our breath away. The sun is bright but not hot—the weather is perfect. A gentle breeze fills our nostrils with the aroma of delicious food. The food is real food. The chairs are real chairs. The aromas, sights, and sounds of the banquet feast before me are unmatched by anything that I had experienced during my life. It is nothing less than delightful. It is a party—it is a celebration of Jesus.

I had hints of this moment before, for the written Word had been here ahead of me. And the written Word and the Living Word are One Word now, one expression of the Living God as they have been for eternity. That which had been foretold is now fulfilled. This is the wedding feast of the Lamb.

> *On this mountain the LORD Almighty will prepare a feast of rich food for all peoples, a banquet of aged wine – the best of meats and the finest of wines.*
>
> —Isaiah 25:6

The Lamb is now unified with His bride, the church. The Redeemer and the redeemed are together forever. It is as it had been written.

> *While they were eating, Jesus took bread, gave thanks and broke it, and gave it to his disciples, saying, "Take and eat; this is my body."*
>
> *Then he took the cup, gave thanks and offered it to them, saying, "Drink from it, all of you. This is my blood of the covenant, which is*

poured out for many for the forgiveness of sins. I tell you, I will not drink of this fruit of the vine from now on <u>until that day when I drink it anew with you in my Father's kingdom."</u>

When they had sung a hymn, they went out to the Mount of Olives.
—Matthew 26:26-30 (emphasis added)

No sooner have I taken my seat than the guest of honor takes His seat right next to me. *Jesus* sits next to *me* at the table! We delight in each other as we enjoy the celebration. As I look around and speak with the rest of the guests—thousands upon thousands of them—I do not see Jesus sitting next to them. At least it does not appear that way to me. But what I cannot see is through their eyes. For through their eyes no one is sitting next to me. And yet seated on the seat next to each of them *they* see their Savior. Not a million little Jesus figures—just one Jesus. For through the additional six dimensions within which we all now eternally exist and interact, this is not just possible but is somehow perfect and complete. It is the way it always should have been.

I am reminded that this is actually the way that it has always been. For all ten of the dimensions had in fact been there all of our lives, just as described in the book of Genesis, just as explained in the ancient Talmudic writings. So much is explained by the full revelation of the other six dimensions. They had in fact served as the intermediary pathways for the many Old and New Testament appearances of angels. The many other unexplained and seemingly mysterious Scriptural incidents, such as the translation in space that Philip had experienced in his interaction with the Ethiopian eunuch, now seem obvious and matter-of-fact in the context of the ten dimensions in which I now experience *real* life.

Of even more significance is that the full ten-dimensional spectrum of God's perfect creation had supplied the corridors for the bodily manifestations of Jesus that had occurred throughout the *Old* Testament writings. And yet, because of the fall, mankind had been capable of interaction in only four dimensions—until now. All of the dimensions that I and all mankind had been created to live in, and that are present and revealed in perfection in the Garden of Eden, are now completely transparent and seamless and so very real. Our interaction with our Savior is now no longer limited to the four dimensions that had made up the totality of our lives.

This multi-dimensional interaction with His created beings is, in fact, the very nature of the personal, intimate relationship that the Savior of millions of people has enjoyed since creation—with every single one of them. The only difference is that now *we can see Him*! Now we all realize that He had, indeed, been right at our sides for every minute of every day of our entire lives on earth—palpably, literally, and *always* right at our sides.

> *For you have been my hope, O Sovereign LORD, my confidence since my youth. From birth I have relied on you; you brought me forth from my mother's womb. I will ever praise you.*
>
> —Psalm 71:5-6 (emphasis added)

He had communicated with us through His Holy Spirit, sometimes indirectly, sometimes very directly. Our experiences of Him had varied between individuals and had been quite variable over the time frame of each of our lives. But now, through our entrance into the full dimensional universe that comprised God's perfect creation, we literally see Him. We actually hear His voice. We feel His touch. We can watch Him chew the piece of fish He is eating right now and we can watch Him drink from the cup of wine that sits before Him on the table. It is perfection.

Jesus now sits next to each of us carrying on a conversation just like a long-lost friend. He speaks of the will of the Father. He speaks of the meal before us. He delights in each of us. And we eat! Just as Jesus had eaten every time He had been with His disciples, so we now eat. And it is more wonderful than I had ever imagined. The extraordinary heightening of my senses and the starkly unconstrained tastes and smells of the banquet feast result in a very human experience. My fear in life that we would all just be spirits floating around in the clouds without physical human bodies had denied the very declaration of God that His physical creation is very good indeed. I now marvel at the fact that the very Son of God has taken on a physical body—human skin—for all eternity.

Now, as Jesus walks to the throne at the front of the magnificent outdoor banquet hall, it appears to each of us that the Jesus we had been speaking with and sitting next to is now going to address the whole group. And He is. He is always with each and every one of us. For this is the reward. *He* is the reward. All is the reward. *"Ruling over ten cities"* is not the reward. Ruling over cities had not been the point during our lives and it is not the point of our eternity. He was the point then and He is the point now. He is the point for eternity. And at this very special feast we delight in Him, for He is, and always has been, our everything.

Now, the moment has arrived to which all else has merely been a prelude, that which had been ordained before time and foretold in the written Word.

Then I saw in the right hand of him who sat on the throne a scroll with writing on both sides and sealed with seven seals. And I saw a mighty angel proclaiming in a loud voice, "Who is worthy to break the seals and open the scroll?"

But no one in heaven or on earth or under the earth could open the scroll or even look inside it.

I wept and wept because no one was found who was worthy to open the scroll or look inside.

Then one of the elders said to me, "Do not weep! See, the Lion of the tribe of Judah, the Root of David, has triumphed. He is able to open the scroll and its seven seals."

Then I saw a Lamb, looking as if it had been slain, standing in the center of the throne, encircled by the four living creatures and the elders. He had seven horns and seven eyes, which are the seven spirits of God sent out into all the earth. He came and took the scroll from the right hand of him who sat on the throne. And when he had taken it, the four living creatures and the twenty-four elders fell down before the Lamb. Each one had a harp and they were holding golden bowls full of incense, which are the prayers of the saints.

—Revelation 5:1-8

And we, every man and every woman of the body of the redeemed church, immediately know the true fulfillment of the Word. The worship begins. Not the worship of the focused total attention that I now give my Savior continually, although this is worship indeed. Instead, it is corporate worship. For now the body of Christ, the bride, is gathered together forever. Our purpose, the eternal purpose of our deep heart, is singular: to focus our attention, as the body of the redeemed, on the Redeemer. We all fall down before Him Who had been slain.

And the singing begins! We sing a song. It is a new song. It is the song of the redeemed. We sing as with one voice, but also as a multitude of voices. There is perfect harmony. It is a perfect blending—yet each voice is distinct. Each voice adds a tone, a harmony, without which the whole would not be the whole; it would be not be complete.

And they sang a new song: "You are worthy to take the scroll and to open its seals, because you were slain, and with your blood you purchased men for God from every tribe and language and people and nation. You have made them to be a kingdom and priests to serve our God, and they will reign on the earth."

Then I looked and heard the voice of many angels, numbering thousands upon thousands, and ten thousand times ten thousand. They encircled the throne and the living creatures and the elders. In a loud voice they sang: "Worthy is the Lamb, who was slain, to receive power and wealth and wisdom and strength and honor and glory and praise!"

Then I heard every creature in heaven and on earth and under the earth and on the sea, and all that is in them, singing: "To him who sits on the throne and to the Lamb be praise and honor and glory and power, for ever and ever!"

—Revelation 5:9-13

We sing as a unified body to the King of kings. Yet we sing as individuals, each on our own, face-to-face with our very personal Redeemer. We sing as one. We sing to Him and to the Father and to the Spirit. We praise Him for who He is. We praise Him for His mercy. We praise Him for His righteousness. We praise Him for His justice. We praise Him for His compassion. We praise Him for His holiness. And we praise Him for His sacrifice. We praise Him for all of those qualities and attributes that are His alone—in infinite proportion. We praise Him for those attributes that are His very nature, any of which, if missing, would declare that He is, in fact, not God.

The worship songs we sang during our lives are all here in the song of the redeemed—every one of them. Every time we had raised our voices in song to the glory of God, it had in fact resonated in eternity. Every song had been written in the mind of the Holy Spirit of the Living God before time began. Each and every one had been harmonious components of this *Song of the Redeemed*. During our lives, each song had struck a chord or a note of the song that we now sing together. But then each song had been so incomplete. Now each is not just completed but is also an essential part of this song we sing. The little premonitions of the glory of God that each song had provided during our lives now splendidly unite and burst into the eternal glory of the worship of the Living God.

Jesus sings over me. He sings over all of us as to His bride, the body of the redeemed. He sings a wedding song. He sings a song of joy. He sings a song of love to the Father and to the Spirit and to each of us. For in the offering of His bride to the Father all is now complete.

> *Then I heard what sounded like a great multitude, like the roar of rushing waters and like loud peals of thunder, shouting: "Hallelujah! For our Lord God Almighty reigns. Let us rejoice and be glad and give him glory! For the wedding of the Lamb has come, and his bride has made herself ready. Fine linen, bright and clean, was given her to wear." (Fine linen stands for the righteous acts of the saints.) Then the angel said to me, "Write: 'Blessed are those who are invited to the wedding supper of the Lamb!'" And he added, "These are the true words of God."*
>
> —Revelation 19:6-9 (emphasis added)

Chapter 11

And the Earth Shone With the Glory of the Lord

The corporate worship of the Lamb by his bride, the banquet song of the redeemed, ends with our unified cry as if with one voice:

> *"Give thanks to the LORD Almighty, for the LORD is good; his love endures forever."*
>
> —*Jeremiah 33:11*

We all watch as the seventh seal is opened. It's opening announces the time of God's wrath upon the earth below. It occurs exactly as it had been written. But now our time as spectators has come to an end. For the Lamb of God now rises to His feet at the right hand of the Father. His head turns, and for a very short time He is silent. It is as if His attention is captured by something He hears. Every eye watches in anticipation. His next action catches me off guard, and yet it really doesn't. For with a single stride He leaps upon a powerful white horse that had been faithfully standing by, anxiously stamping the ground in anticipation of what lay ahead.

Now we also hear what He had first heard. Heard first by Him because it is the cry of His very heart. It is that for which He had been waiting for two thousand years. Now, we all hear it together. It is as if a symphony of voices is crying out simultaneously as a single voice. The words are clear and distinct. It is exactly as it had been foretold so long before:

> *"I myself said, "'How gladly would I treat you like sons and give you a desirable land, the most beautiful inheritance of any nation.' I thought you would call me 'Father' and not turn away from following me. But like a woman unfaithful to her husband, so you have been unfaithful to me, O house of Israel," declares the LORD.*

A cry is heard on the barren heights, the weeping and pleading of the people of Israel, because they have perverted their ways and have forgotten the LORD their God.

"Return, faithless people; I will cure you of backsliding."

"Yes, we will come to you, for you are the LORD our God. Surely the [idolatrous] commotion on the hills and mountains is a deception; surely in the LORD our God is the salvation of Israel.

From our youth shameful gods have consumed the fruits of our fathers' labor—their flocks and herds, their sons and daughters. Let us lie down in our shame, and let our disgrace cover us. We have sinned against the LORD our God, both we and our fathers; from our youth till this day we have not obeyed the LORD our God."
—Jeremiah 3:19-25 (emphasis added)

Now the Jewish people cry out. They had not recognized their Messiah when He had first ridden triumphant through their streets. Their sin had led to blindness.

"Hear, you deaf; look, you blind, and see! Who is blind but my servant, and deaf like the messenger I send? Who is blind like the one committed to me, blind like the servant of the LORD? You have seen many things, but have paid no attention; your ears are open, but you hear nothing."

Who handed Jacob over to become loot, and Israel to the plunderers? Was it not the LORD, against whom we have sinned? For they would not follow his ways; they did not obey his law. So he poured out on them his burning anger, the violence of war. It enveloped them in flames, yet they did not understand; it consumed them, but they did not take it to heart.
—Isaiah 42:18-20, 24-25

But now it is the will of God that the eyes of His people be opened. And He, *"the Holy One of Israel, [their] Savior" (Isaiah 42:3),* will turn the darkness into light.

I will lead the blind by ways they have not known, along unfamiliar paths I will guide them; I will turn the darkness into light before them and make the rough places smooth. These are the things I will do; I will not forsake them.

—Isaiah 42:16

Repentance fills their hearts as the Spirit of God whirls through the remnant of God's chosen people—just as had been predicted. The Lord held nothing back in His revelation of the things to come. The Jewish remnant, those of His very own beloved people who wholeheartedly seek the Lord, are now filled with the Holy Spirit.

"In those days, at that time," declares the LORD, "the people of Israel and the people of Judah together will go in tears to seek the LORD their God. They will ask the way to Zion and turn their faces toward it. They will come and bind themselves to the LORD in an everlasting covenant that will not be forgotten.

—Jeremiah 50:4-5

They cry out to Him and He responds with love, mercy, and forgiveness just as He had promised.

"In those days, at that time," declares the LORD, "search will be made for Israel's guilt, but there will be none, and for the sins of Judah, but none will be found, for I will forgive the remnant I spare."
—Jeremiah 50:20 (emphasis added)

By His holy will, we the redeemed are as one. We are simultaneously filled with the knowledge of what we are to do. The hidden remnant of God's people is not just in danger—it faces annihilation. His chosen remnant now lies threatened in the midst of their repentance by an enemy of old. We know this enemy and we know his followers. We know them by the name assigned them in the written Word. We know their fate and our part in that preordained fate. The forces of darkness have ruled the earth, but the time of their end is at hand.

The noise of battle is in the land, the noise of great destruction! How broken and shattered is the hammer of the whole earth! How desolate is Babylon among the nations! I set a trap for you, O Babylon, and you were caught before you knew it; you were found and captured because you opposed the LORD.

The LORD has opened his arsenal and brought out the weapons of his wrath, for the Sovereign LORD Almighty has work to do in the land of the Babylonians. Come against her from afar. Break open her granaries; pile her up like heaps of grain. Completely destroy her and leave her no remnant. Kill all her young bulls; let them go down to the slaughter! Woe to them! For their day has come, the time for them to be punished. Listen to the fugitives and refugees from Babylon declaring in Zion how the LORD our God has taken vengeance, vengeance for his temple.

"Summon archers against Babylon, all those who draw the bow. Encamp all around her; let no one escape. Repay her for her deeds; do to her as she has done. For she has defied the LORD, the Holy One of Israel. Therefore, her young men will fall in the streets; all her soldiers will be silenced in that day," declares the LORD.

"See, I am against you, O arrogant one," declares the Lord, the LORD Almighty, "for your day has come, the time for you to be punished. The arrogant one will stumble and fall and no one will help her up; I will kindle a fire in her towns that will consume all who are around her."

—Jeremiah 50:22-32 (emphasis added)

At the sound of His battle cry, Jesus' horse snorts in unrestrained anticipation as it rears up on its hind legs and plunges through the glowing clouds of the Shekinah glory into the sky below. The plan of the Messiah is of old and it is clear to all.

The LORD will restore the splendor of Jacob like the splendor of Israel, though destroyers have laid them waste and have ruined their vines.

—Nahum 2:2

The Bride of Christ knows well that it has begun. The day of days is upon us—and upon the nations of the earth below. With a single word God's will is to be done—but, not without us.

For it is God's will that we the redeemed are to accompany Jesus through the clouds below. Our inclusion in this quest most certainly is not a question of God's capability, of His strength or His faithfulness to do exactly what He promised—or of His need for anyone's help. He had repeatedly and purposefully demonstrated

His ability to conquer throughout the battles of the Old Testament—for the glory of conquest is always His. But, as I now remember, God rarely chose to do it all Himself. He had always allowed His angels or His saints to be the mechanism, the instrument, of His wrathful interventions. And so it is today on this day of days. His day of days is to also be our day of days. We delight in this revelation, for our hearts are totally His and our fervor for His righteousness is white hot by the hand of the continually indwelling Spirit of God.

> *Your troops will be willing on your day of battle. Arrayed in holy majesty, from the womb of the dawn you will receive the dew of your youth.*
>
> —Psalm 110:3 (emphasis added)

What a stunning moment it is. In all of creation there has been nothing like this. For now, just as promised, the earth is immediately and unmistakably filled with the very glory of His essence:

> *For the earth will be filled with the knowledge of the glory of the LORD, as the waters cover the sea.*
>
> —Habakkuk 2:14

And *we* are going to war as the armies of the Living God.

Chapter 12

The Task At Hand

Simultaneously with the Lamb's mounting of His white horse, every individual member of the unified body of the *Redeemed*, the glorified bride of the Glorified One, immediately turn toward their assigned positions in the armies of the Living God. Each of us knows exactly where to go and we proceed with the excitement that accompanies a long-anticipated event. Our positions were assigned to us before the beginning of time. Despite our ignorance of the significance of our feelings then, we had lived it, anticipated it, and had enjoyed intermittent reflections of it repeatedly during our lives on earth. In those moments, when a ray of light from eternity had flickered through the clouds of the "reality" of our lives, we had recognized it as something special, as something *set apart*, as something of very special, albeit unknown, significance. We had bathed in its holy warmth for the fleeting moment of its enigmatic unveiling. After it had passed, in our hearts we had known it as something very extraordinary, as truth in a very untrue world. And we had marveled at its hold on us and at the immediacy of its capture of our hearts.

During our lives, these moments had always rapidly faded away. Almost as soon as the knowledge of the Holy opened like a ray of light through the clouds, it would be gone. For then we had, by God's divine purpose, been given only intermittent short glimpses of our positions, our tasks, our functions, in this great army now assembled in the swirling clouds of the Shekinah glory above the mountains east of Jerusalem.

Now there is no blurring of our vision by the clouds of sin, pride, and materialism. Our idols are gone. Our eyes are open. Our vision was made whole by the appearance of the Lamb. We have become *"like Him."* We can see all now. Just as promised, the night is over; morning is here.

And there is work to be done.

Oh yes, to our shear delight, there is still work to do in this next life. There are still arduous tasks after passing through the portal of what had been referred to as the first death. For the Word clearly taught that God had created work as a good thing. It had been only after the fall of man that it had become "work" as I had known it during my life. But now the task, the work, is pure and undefiled. In this—its original state—it is remarkably different from all I that had experienced during my life.

Actually, it is not the work that is different. In many respects it seems very similar—equally difficult and equally challenging—just as it was during my life. But now, somehow, it is just simply wonderful. No, the work is not different. My approach to it is what has changed. For there had been such a transformation when I had first laid eyes on the Lamb. During my life on earth I had approached work correctly only intermittently, and then only by the grace of God—certainly not by my own effort. I well remember those times. I had been confronted with a difficult task, an overwhelming task like the one that now stands before us all. It was one that I knew I had no chance of dealing with on my own. I had turned to God and asked for wisdom.

> *Consider it pure joy, my brothers, whenever you face trials of many kinds, because you know that the testing of your faith develops perseverance. Perseverance must finish its work so that you may be mature and complete, not lacking anything.*
>
> *If any of you lacks wisdom, he should ask God, who gives generously to all without finding fault, and it will be given to him. But when he asks, he must believe and not doubt, because he who doubts is like a wave of the sea, blown and tossed by the wind. That man should not think he will receive anything from the Lord; he is a double-minded man, unstable in all he does.*
>
> —James 1:2-8 (emphasis added)

I knew in my heart that God had defined a path through each episode of my life before time began. I knew that God had promised to be there whenever I remembered to ask and when I was wholeheartedly committed to following through with the solution that God handed me, whether I liked it or not. Wholehearted commitment to the will of God in my life was the key. It meant turning to God first rather than trying to solve the problem on my own with the so-called *wisdom* of the world. It meant trusting God.

Now, after the transformation that occurred when I first saw Jesus, things are different. The work, the tasks, the arduous endeavors, and the challenges are all still there. But now I am in continual communion with the Living God. Continual. This means that my *first* instantaneous thought when confronted with each and every new challenge—all sent by God just as they had been during my life—is to turn immediately to God, to seek God's will and strength in the situation. In this I find total fulfillment, for this glorification of God by turning to Him in each and every situation—this is that for which I was made. It is simply thrilling. There is no thought to turning to Jesus, I just do it, automatically, continually, every time. In this, my heart is totally committed to the will of God. There is no blindness or blurry vision of God's will. There is no half-hearted commitment to its completion in my life. There is simply no room for being double-minded.

Now the tasks are still delivered up by my loving God. But now my first thought is of God's will in the matter. My automatic first request is for God's strength. My mandatory prayer, for my heart has no room for anything else, is for my only best friend Jesus to accompany me on the adventure set before me.

There is no question about the immediate task at hand. There is no confusion. There is no anxiety. There certainly is no fear. The fear has been completely removed. Fear is not even a possibility now, for I now stand continually in the presence of God. I always have. It has just never been the totality, the summation, of my experience as it is now.

In this state—of being in the continual Presence of God—we all know His will and move *as one* swiftly toward our assigned positions for the first task of eternity. It is a task clearly defined before time began and described to the detail in the Word of God to man.

There is a job to be done.

This is not just a little task to tidy things up a bit. Oh no. This is the fulfillment of all that was promised. This is the culmination of the battle that has waged for centuries on the earth and in the heavens above. This is the righting of every wrong.

> The LORD is a jealous and avenging God; the LORD takes vengeance
> and is filled with wrath. The LORD takes <u>vengeance on his foes</u> and
> <u>maintains his wrath against his enemies</u>. The LORD is slow to anger
> and great in power; the LORD <u>will not leave the guilty unpunished</u>.
> His way is in the whirlwind and the storm, and clouds are the dust of
> his feet.

—Nahum 1:2-3 (emphasis added)

This battle is nothing less than the completion of all prophecy. This is the balancing of all accounts by Almighty God. And we, His redeemed, are to be the instruments of His wrath.

> *Praise the LORD. Sing to the LORD a new song, his praise in the assembly of the saints. Let Israel rejoice in their Maker; let the people of Zion be glad in their King. Let them praise his name with dancing and make music to him with tambourine and harp. For the LORD takes delight in his people; he crowns the humble with salvation. Let the saints rejoice in this honor and sing for joy on their beds.*
>
> <u>*May the praise of God be in their mouths and a double-edged sword in their hands, to inflict vengeance on the nations and punishment on the peoples, to bind their kings with fetters, their nobles with shackles of iron, to carry out the sentence written against them. This is the glory of all his saints.*</u> *Praise the LORD.*
>
> —Psalm 149 (emphasis added)

This is indeed the long-awaited answer to the prayers of the righteous recorded in the Psalms of God. This is battle. The opening of the scroll by the Lamb is past now. The seals have all been opened. The wrath has been poured out and awaits its culmination in the final stroke of the fury of the winepress of the wrath of the Mighty God. It is time for war.

Now the mighty armies, gathered under the man of perdition, the antichrist, stand amassed in the deserts of Iraq and Jordan. They are poised to strike, coiled and straining, swallowed up in the anticipation of their final battle preparation. They will hit the remnant of Israel hiding in Basra.

> *For out of Jerusalem will come a remnant, and out of Mount Zion a band of survivors. The zeal of the LORD Almighty will accomplish this.*
>
> —Isaiah 37:32

The harried flight of the Jewish remnant to Basra had immediately followed the *abomination of desolations* that had occurred in the temple in Jerusalem 3 1/2 years earlier. Satan, in his fury, had then pursued the Jewish faithful.

Therefore rejoice, you heavens and you who dwell in them! But woe to the earth and the sea, because the devil has gone down to you! He is filled with fury, because he knows that his time is short." When the dragon saw that he had been hurled to the earth, he pursued the woman who had given birth to the male child.

—Revelation 12:12-13 (emphasis added)

On that frightful day of the abomination, none of the remnant had gone *"back to get his cloak..."*

"So when you see standing in the holy place 'the abomination that causes desolation,' spoken of through the prophet Daniel—let the reader understand—then let those who are in Judea flee to the mountains. Let no one on the roof of his house go down to take anything out of the house. Let no one in the field go back to get his cloak."

—Matthew 24:15-18

And God, ever faithful to His Word, had preserved them against the armies of the antichrist as Satan had hunted them in his fury.

The woman was given the two wings of a great eagle, so that she might fly to the place prepared for her in the desert, where she would be taken care of for a time, times and half a time, out of the serpent's reach.

—Revelation 12:14

But now the armies of darkness had found their prey. By divine determination they had been given the location of the remnant they had sought. Although their response was predictable, the intensity—the fervor—that was the hallmark of their efforts was not. Never before has so ruthless an army been gathered on the face of the earth as now swirls into position in the desert sands surrounding Basra. Only the most elite guard units of the armies of the antichrist have been chosen for this most important of tasks. They are massively and powerfully armed with awesome weapons of destruction, for their preparation was complete, planned even before the beginning of time. The soldiers of eternal darkness now stand in their machines of war ready to unleash the dark power of the one in whose name they gather. They are unified in purpose. That purpose is to make war against the very remnant of the chosen people of Israel—the very remnant of God.

The preparation of their minds is also complete, for they have—to the man—given themselves over completely to this man-beast whom they now unconditionally follow. They have completely and without reservation turned away from God, away from the very zenith of their creation. God has, as He promised in His Word, turned them over to the decadence and depravity of their minds. Now they rail angrily against God. They lash out at all who stand in their way, all who dare to oppose them and the new world they envision, the new world that will follow the destruction of the Jews and the defeat of Jesus. They will fight against God Himself. They believe they can win. Such is the deception of their unchallenged leader, the incarnate summation of evil. He is there on the battlefield with them to remind them that victory will soon be theirs. He will lead this battle himself.

The purpose of their preparation is visible, singular: the complete and final destruction of the last of the Jews. This battle is to be their grand finale. It is to be nothing less than the complete elimination of those who they believe have plagued their cause for centuries—a goal spoken about by their kind since Isaac and Ishmael. For this is the desire of the darkness they follow. They share his eternally damned anger. They share his fury. They share his passion for destruction, his lust for the very last drop of Jewish blood. They recognize no standard except his. They recognize no law except that which flies in the face of the God they so furiously rebel against. These people, this remnant that they now surround, are God's chosen ones, and their destruction represents nothing less than a chance to strike out against the Almighty God who torments them. The destruction of the remnant is their sole purpose, their only thought, and their consuming passion.

With this as their purpose, and the antichrist's command as their only allegiance, they now roll in their machines of war toward the area of the desert that had remained hidden from them for so long. What they cannot know, cannot comprehend, is that they will never get there. Indeed, the revelation of the existence and exact location of the hiding place of the remnant had been held from them for an eternity and its unveiling at this late time seems so fortuitous—almost planned.

The woman fled into the desert to a place prepared for her by God, where she might be taken care of for 1,260 days.
—Revelation 12:6

All of the redeemed know of the gathering of the armies of Satan, as well as their full intent. And we know exactly the role we are to play in the outcome of this *day of days.* It has all been written and is now permanently and indelibly emblazoned in our minds and on our hearts by the Author of this great drama.

We know that He, the One upon whom we all fix our vision, could end it all with a simple thought, a single word. There is no question of His omnipotence. But the reward of the faithful is now the privilege of His servants—to carry out His will and His Word, to fulfill His prophecy.

> *I have commanded my holy ones; I have summoned my warriors to carry out my wrath—those who rejoice in my triumph. Listen, a noise on the mountains, like that of a great multitude! Listen, an uproar among the kingdoms, like nations massing together! The LORD Almighty is mustering an army for war. They come from faraway lands, from the ends of the heavens—the LORD and the weapons of his wrath—to destroy the whole country.*
>
> —Isaiah 13:3-5 (emphasis added)

Now the battle will unfold by the hand of God's servants. His *saved*, every man and every woman of His church, are His warriors now. This battle is His and it is ours. Surely the victory is totally by the cross of Christ—His strength, His Word, His sacrifice, His suffering, His perseverance, His love, His judgment, His justice, and His power. And yet just as we share with Jesus—by His grace—in the sufferings and victory of the cross, so also will we share in this final great battle.

For the battle is ours to fight.

Jesus, ever at my side, now speaks the words of *"the revelation of Jesus Christ, which God gave him to show his servants what must soon take place."*

> *I saw heaven standing open and there before me was a white horse, whose rider is called Faithful and True. With justice he judges and makes war. His eyes are like blazing fire, and on his head are many crowns. He has a name written on him that no one knows but he himself. He is dressed in a robe dipped in blood, and his name is the Word of God.*
>
> *The armies of heaven were following him, riding on white horses and dressed in fine linen, white and clean.*

Out of his mouth comes a sharp sword with which to strike down the nations. "He will rule them with an iron scepter." He treads the winepress of the fury of the wrath of God Almighty. On his robe and on his thigh he has this name written: KING OF KINGS AND LORD OF LORDS. And I saw an angel standing in the sun, who cried in a loud voice to all the birds flying in midair, "Come, gather together for the great supper of God, so that you may eat the flesh of kings, generals, and mighty men, of horses and their riders, and the flesh of all people, free and slave, small and great." Then I saw the beast and the kings of the earth and their armies gathered together to make war against the rider on the horse <u>and his army</u>.

But the beast was captured, and with him the false prophet who had performed the miraculous signs on his behalf. With these signs he had deluded those who had received the mark of the beast and worshiped his image. The two of them were thrown alive into the fiery lake of burning sulfur. The rest of them were killed with the sword that came out of the mouth of the rider on the horse, and all the birds gorged themselves on their flesh.

—Revelation 19:11-21 (emphasis added)

His almighty decree is succinct, complete, and to the point. But the battle still must be fought. Now our zeal for Him and for His Word fills our every fiber, and the defeat of His enemies is our only thought. For now we know the very thoughts of Jesus. His heart and His mind and His will and this battle are now our all-consuming passion.

Chapter 13

Apache

Somehow, I know exactly where I am going. Jesus and I walk directly toward the hulking figure before us in the clouds above the mountains just east of Jerusalem. It is one of many such figures that are gradually becoming visible in the eerie early light of the day that is dawning in the peaks below. As I move closer I can see its curving wings and tail. In the mist that is burning away in the first rays of light it appears jet black in color and ominous in form. It is a large menacing figure. Somehow, I know every detail of its shape despite the fact that I have never laid eyes on it before. It loosely resembles a shape that I had found strangely alluring during the latter days of my life. It is the shape of an attack helicopter, an *Apache* gunship. I could not help but smile at Jesus who confirms, "Yes. It was Me all along. And, yes, it is all yours!"

I look back at the shadowy image in the shared joy of my Savior—for everything is shared with Him now. I cannot help but stare at the dark intimidating figure of the gunship before me. The day is fully breaking and I can see the details of the ship now in the early light of morning. Surely the *Apache* gunships I had seen during my life had just been hazy premonitions of the ship that stands before me now. This ship is markedly different and yet so eerily familiar. The matte black graphite material from which its armored skin is seamlessly formed is the only color that is visible. Its shape is somehow pleasing and perfect like the feeling one has when staring at utter perfection. It is the perfect completion of that which I had so admired in its incomplete state during my life. Although it is clearly machine-like, it more resembles a living creature—almost like an eagle or a viper…or both? Or possibly it's a dragon, a figure of the imagination. But ominous and menacing it is, and so foreboding of the power that will be unleashed from it so very shortly. Unknown weapons are slung beneath its wings and project from its nose. They are unknown, yet also known. I have, of course, never seen them before. But somehow I know them well, how they work and exactly what they can do.

I climb into the cockpit just as I had imagined myself doing countless times during my life. God had given me flickering glimpses of this moment before. Images that had triggered something in me, that had made me stop and look back a second time every time I had seen in person, in picture, or in film an *Apache* attack helicopter.

I now know that it was not the curves and hollows of its three-dimensional shape themselves that had touched such a deep part of my heart then. Instead it had been the Spirit of the Living God Who had made the weapon-laden, gun-slinging silhouette of an *Apache* gunship flying low over the dunes of the Iraqi desert grab me in such an eternal fashion. I had not known why, but images of the unleashed firepower of these helicopters had always resonated in the deepest reaches of my consciousness.

And now the beast in which I am sitting cradles and encloses around me in a perfect fit. I have never flown this machine before. In fact, I had never flown anything during my life. And yet I feel as if I have flown it a thousand times. It is immediately responsive to my every intention. We are one. I move my fingers in the molded controls that now engulf my hands and every functional part of this flying machine responds reflexively to my every thought and movement. It is as if it had been designed specifically for me.

It is time. My eyes remain fixed on the only One who matters. For now there is nothing else of even trivial importance to me. Only Jesus. At the same time, by the direct command of the One upon whom my eyes are fixed, I *will* the flying machine to lift slowly and deliberately from the ground. I move into the formation of similar hovering beasts that is slowly lifting alongside my *Apache* at the nonverbal command of the King of kings. It is an attack formation. I know exactly where I belong among the slowly turning war machines.

Now we all move as one. And we are not alone. I can see that many other squadrons of flying beasts have similarly lifted from the ground. They also have the appearance of strange living creatures that resemble the war machines of many different ages and many different peoples. Similarly, ground assault troops and battle machines—most resembling the main battle tanks of the armies of many different eras—move forward on the ground below. High-flying *fast-movers* above also accompany our formations of low-flying beasts. We all move as one because we share the mind of Jesus. All are individuals but are somehow united in mind, spirit, will, purpose—and somehow in flesh—with the Lamb. For all are united with Jesus as predicted.

"For this reason a man will leave his father and mother and be united to his wife, and the two will become one flesh." This is a profound mystery—but I am talking about Christ and the church.
—Ephesians 5:31-32 (emphasis added)

Indeed, the Church, the bride of Christ, is united as one flesh and one mind with Jesus. We are all continually in His presence. We continually stand before Him and with Him and united in Him. His mind and thoughts and will are simultaneously ours now, just as His had been one with the Father when He had walked upon the earth. The Spirit is over and in all. Jesus sits beside me in my war machine, just as He sits beside every man and every woman commanding every machine that flies high or rolls low across the desert. Not a whole bunch of little Jesus figures—just one Jesus. We are all connected through the ten dimensions that we now share. At the same time that Jesus is sitting or marching with each individual, He is talking and encouraging and planning and revealing as we go. Jesus is with each of us individually, yet all as one. Such is the multi-dimensional reality of our new bodies and our new existence in Him.

I glance above me and below me at the other elements of the armies of the Living God. Above are many different fast moving flying machines that also have the appearance of living creatures. They resemble the aircraft that have been flown by many different generations of pilots from many different nations. It is like a grand menagerie of airplanes that mirrors the history of flight since mankind first took to the air. Some I recognize, most I do not. Each different type of plane must have piqued the interest of those who saw them back then—and pilot them now—just as the *Apache* had caught mine.

I see one group of swept-back figures that resemble a plummeting falcon—or is it an ominous black bat? They look so familiar. I remember them from my lifetime. They are very much like the F-14 *Tomcat* fighters that I had seen pictures of— perched with their wings folded, almost sulking, upon an aircraft carrier's deck.

And how my brother, Jonathan, had loved them. It had been his one dream in his late adult life to someday fly an F-14. How they had captivated him! They had brought something out in him, something special, and he knew it. They had clearly been a premonition of the brute that he now flies—to his heart's utter delight. These aircraft had been machines in our lifetime, but somehow they seem alive now. For the whole of God's creation seems alive now. These *fast movers* overhead are pulsating and vibrant, with shiny translucent metallic material as skin. They are mechanical, but somehow they are also alive. How they fly! They are fast movers, indeed. Totally responsive to their drivers and so very imposing in their formations above.

And below me are the foot soldiers. They are God's ground assault troops. The armored cavalry, comprised of many different rolling war machines, accompany them. All are in formation; all are armed. The weapons of these warriors fit their new roles as they had imagined them in their lives—weapons, roles, and lives that span the history of mankind. For the armies of the Living God are comprised of men and women from every era, from every nation, from every people. All now fulfill the roles, carry the weapons and man the machines that had set their imaginations on fire during their lives. In every man and in every woman there had been a warrior. God had sent those momentary hints of eternity to tell them of His plans for them. They had all experienced intriguing premonitions of the roles they now play in the battle of all battles. And the One who had spoken so deeply to their hearts back then, Jesus, now accompanies each of them into battle.

Chapter 14

Sons

My sons, William, Ryan, and Michael had grown up with a fascination for hand-to-hand combat. Their favorite scenes from their favorite movies had all been the same. They were the scenes where a single warrior was pitted in desperate battle against a super-enemy warrior, or single-handedly against many soldiers of the armies of evil. The *Star Wars* light-saber duel between the Jedi knights and the evil Darth Mal had been a favorite. The massive battle scenes of all three of the *Lord of the Rings Trilogy* had been others. I had watched each one of my sons so many times in the back yard, each with stick sword in hand, taking on the hoards of evil warriors from the armies of the dark side. In all cases it had been the same—my sons pitted in mortal combat against vast numbers of enraged, evil, powerful warriors in the throes of desperate battle.

Back then, of course they knew that the movie scenes they mimicked were all imaginary. They thought that such victories against such overwhelming odds had never really happened. They thought that these scenes were all a product of an overactive Hollywood imagination. They all knew the Lord and they all knew, and had experienced, the willingness of Almighty God to intervene in their lives in a non-subtle fashion. But these guys were wiping out dozens of the evil warriors at a time in these movie scenes. "That couldn't really happen…could it, Dad?"

The grin of great anticipation that had come across my face at this question had perplexed them until our family Bible reading that night. I remember well that I could hardly wait. I knew exactly what the scriptural passage would be that night. In 2 Samuel 23 are words that their hearts longed to hear, for they speak of "*David's Mighty Men.*"

> *These are the names of David's mighty men: Josheb-basshebeth, a Tahkemonite, was chief of the Three; he raised his spear against eight hundred men, whom he killed in one encounter.*
>
> *Next to him was Eleazar son of Dodai the Ahohite. As one of the three mighty men, he was with David when they taunted the Philistines*

gathered [at Pas Dammim] for battle. Then the men of Israel retreated, <u>but he stood his ground and struck down the Philistines till his hand grew tired and froze to the sword. The LORD brought about a great victory that day. The troops returned to Eleazar, but only to strip the dead.</u>

Next to him was Shammah son of Agee the Hararite. When the Philistines banded together at a place where there was a field full of lentils, Israel's troops fled from them. <u>But Shammah took his stand in the middle of the field. He defended it and struck the Philistines down, and the LORD brought about a great victory</u>.

—2Samuel 23:8-12 (emphasis added)

Abishai the brother of Joab son of Zeruiah was chief of the Three. <u>He raised his spear against three hundred men, whom he killed</u>, and so he became as famous as the Three. Was he not held in greater honor than the Three? He became their commander, even though he was not included among them.

—2Samuel 23:18-19 (emphasis added)

Before I read those passages that night, I reminded them all of one thing. Despite the fact that it was God Who carried the day in every one of the circumstances that we were going to read about, these mighty men still had to step forward into battle and *actually fight the fight.*

It is that way in nearly every book of the Bible. The pattern is consistent. The mighty malevolent foe stands before the nation of Israel or before the individual godly warrior. This enemy is evil incarnate. The godly warrior turns to God for strength and God's decree is that His warrior will be triumphant. But, and let there be no question about it, the battle always has to be fought—either by His Israelite warrior or by His warrior angels. The individual chosen by God to be His instrument of wrath always has to pick up a weapon and, by the power of the Living God, take the fight to the enemy.

I had closely watched my sons' faces as I began to read the passages. As I continued to read, it became obvious to me that my boys were no longer in our family hearth room with their parents. Their eyes were glazed over and gazed into the scenes that now played out in their hearts and minds. I knew that these passages from the Word of God had hit home. I knew that they had resonated in the hidden, secret places of their young warrior hearts. My sons had been designed that way. They are warriors as their God had decreed, and to hear that the very exploits they dreamed of had actually taken place, and that it had been at the decree of the very Lord whom they so actively sought, delighted them to the very deep parts of their young hearts.

Now I see them below me as I fly with the *Apache* formation. That which had been merely a fleeting glimpse during their lives is now the first very real reality of their eternity. Their Savior walks beside them, speaking to each of them individually. He is singing His praise over them. He tells them of the exploits of His mighty men and tells them that they are now in that very elite group. They are His mighty men.

> *Together they will be like mighty men trampling the muddy streets in battle. Because the LORD is with them, they will fight and overthrow the horsemen.*
> —Zechariah 10:5

He tells them of the enemy ahead and the plan for the battle. He is going into battle at their sides and He will have their backs. There is no fear among them, only the anticipation of what lays ahead.

> *The LORD will march out like a mighty man, like a warrior he will stir up his zeal; with a shout he will raise the battle cry and will triumph over his enemies.*
> —Isaiah 42:13

Chapter 15

Streaming From Heaven Above

The time for battle is upon us and Jesus is the first to battle. He alone leads the onslaught from above. The enemy below never knew what hit them. Astride His champion white steed, He blasts down through the glowing clouds of the Shekinah glory with a deafening thunderclap heard by every man, woman, and child on Earth. Like a magnificent yet furious tempest, the whole of the armies of the Living God stream down behind Him. Together we descend rapidly through the sky above the Mount of Olives just east of Jerusalem.

> *I saw heaven standing open and there before me was a white horse, whose rider is called Faithful and True. With justice he judges and makes war. His eyes are like blazing fire, and on his head are many crowns. He has a name written on him that no one knows but he himself. He is dressed in a robe dipped in blood, and his name is the Word of God.*
>
> *The armies of heaven were following him, riding on white horses and dressed in fine linen, white and clean. Out of his mouth comes a sharp sword with which to strike down the nations. "He will rule them with an iron scepter." He treads the winepress of the fury of the wrath of God Almighty. On his robe and on his thigh he has this name written: KING OF KINGS AND LORD OF LORDS.*
> —Revelation 19:11-16 (emphasis added)

Jesus appears instantaneously—as the very glory of God—to every nation on earth. All of His redeemed follow close behind in a flowing, ever widening battle formation behind the single figure Who is the point of the battle formation and the point of it all. He is seen by all. None on earth are exempt.

> *The LORD will lay bare his holy arm in the sight of all the nations, and all the ends of the earth will see the salvation of our God.*
> —Isaiah 52:10 (emphasis added)

Every eye gazes upon His face. Simultaneously, instantaneously, all behold the visage that had been stored deep in the untraveled back roads of their hearts. For He had planted the knowledge of God in all of their hearts before time began.

To some His appearance signals nothing less than the most joyous magnificent rescue of all rescues, eclipsing every vivid image of every desperate rescue they had seen played out in their lives. The cry of their hearts has been heard and their rescue is at hand. When all had seemed hopeless and lost, when the most horribly dreaded nightmare of their darkest imagination had been crashing down around them like an unstoppable avalanche, and when they had cried out in the futile despair that is known only by those who are utterly and dreadfully and desperately alone—then He appears! The tables are now turned and from their despair springs hope and from that hope, eternal joy.

> *Look, there on the mountains, the feet of one who brings good news, who proclaims peace! Celebrate your festivals, O Judah, and fulfill your vows. No more will the wicked invade you; they will be completely destroyed.*
> —Nahum 1:15 (emphasis added)

Yet to others this is the horror of horrors. As they stand complacent and content in their lives *"eating and drinking, marrying and giving in marriage"* (Matthew 24:38) and when all seems so secure in their position in the world—He appears.

> *Look, he is coming with the clouds, and every eye will see him, even those who pierced him; and all the peoples of the earth will mourn because of him. So shall it be! Amen.*
> —Revelation 1:7 (emphasis added)

In an instant they know that every terror that they had dreaded since their first breath had been mere premonitions of the unsounded depth of the infinite awfulness that now overwhelms them like a tidal wave of pure horror. For in a single instant they now know the reality of the justice and judgment that is embodied by the God of all creation.

> *The LORD is good, a refuge in times of trouble. He cares for those who trust in him, but with an overwhelming flood he will make an end of [Nineveh]; he will pursue his foes into darkness. Whatever they plot against the LORD he will bring to an end; trouble will not come a second time. They will be entangled among thorns and drunk from*

their wine; they will be consumed like dry stubble. From you, [O Nineveh,] has one come forth who plots evil against the LORD and counsels wickedness. This is what the LORD says: "Although they have allies and are numerous, they will be cut off and pass away. Although I have afflicted you, [O Judah,] I will afflict you no more. Now I will break their yoke from your neck and tear your shackles away." The LORD has given a command concerning you, [Nineveh]: "You will have no descendants to bear your name. I will destroy the carved images and cast idols that are in the temple of your gods. I will prepare your grave, for you are vile."

An attacker advances against you, [Nineveh]. Guard the fortress, watch the road, brace yourselves, marshal all your strength!
—Nahum 1:7-14; 2:1 (emphasis added)

They see us, the legions of the armies of the Living God, in full battle array. We, in our multitudes of flying and rolling and marching formations, stream behind Jesus. We are accompanied by the thunderous roar of our war machines.

See, the LORD is coming with fire, and his chariots are like a whirlwind; he will bring down his anger with fury, and his rebuke with flames of fire. For with fire and with his sword the LORD will execute judgment upon all men, and many will be those slain by the LORD.
—Isaiah 66:15-16 (emphasis added)

It is an incredible sight—like nothing that has ever been seen in the history of mankind. The sudden appearance of Jesus immediately and completely overwhelms every other concern that had—just a moment before—seemed so very important.

Wail, for the day of the LORD is near; it will come like destruction from the Almighty. Because of this, all hands will go limp, every man's heart will melt. Terror will seize them, pain and anguish will grip them; they will writhe like a woman in labor. They will look aghast at each other, their faces aflame.

See, the day of the LORD is coming—a cruel day, with wrath and fierce anger—to make the land desolate and destroy the sinners within it.

—Isaiah 13:6-9 (emphasis added)

Though it catches them all off guard, deep in their hearts they know exactly what is occurring. For every man, woman, and child have always somehow known. For the Word of God is written on their hearts also. They have been told everything, even to the very detail of sight and sound.

> *Blow the trumpet in Zion; sound the alarm on my holy hill. Let all who live in the land tremble, for <u>the day of the LORD is coming</u>. It is close at hand—a day of darkness and gloom, a day of clouds and blackness. <u>Like dawn spreading across the mountains a large and mighty army comes, such as never was of old nor ever will be in ages to come</u>.*
>
> *Before them fire devours, behind them a flame blazes. Before them the land is like the garden of Eden, behind them, a desert waste— nothing escapes them. <u>They have the appearance of horses; they gallop along like cavalry. With a noise like that of chariots they leap over the mountaintops, like a crackling fire consuming stubble, like a mighty army drawn up for battle. At the sight of them, nations are in anguish; every face turns pale</u>.*
>
> —Joel 2:1-6 (emphasis added)
>
> *Before them the earth shakes, the sky trembles, the sun and moon are darkened, and the stars no longer shine.*
>
> *<u>The LORD thunders at the head of his army; his forces are beyond number, and mighty are those who obey his command</u>. The day of the LORD is great; <u>it is dreadful. Who can endure it?</u>*
>
> —Joel 2:10-11 (emphasis added)

As promised, *"the kings of the earth, the princes, the generals, the rich, the mighty, and every slave and every free man…"(*Revelation 6:15) know, and they know absolutely, that the voice of the One that had cried out to them from the deepest recesses of their hearts is real. All that they had ignored is true. All that they feared is upon them.

> *The mountains quake before him and the hills melt away. The earth trembles at his presence, the world and all who live in it. Who can*

withstand his indignation? Who can endure his fierce anger? His wrath is poured out like fire; the rocks are shattered before him.

—Nahum 1:5-6

Still, in their hearts they do not believe. They do not acknowledge what they know is true, that resistance truly is futile. There is no hope for it. Their stubborn minds will not, cannot, allow them to turn to Him to repent and humble themselves. They have spent the whole of their lives ignoring and turning away from His beckoning call. They have become calloused to it. It all seems like irrelevant gibberish to them. Their hearts have become impenetrably hardened by their habitual following of the commands of the world instead of those of God.

So instead of falling on their faces before Him now, they turn toward the storm descending from the eastern sky and gnash their teeth. They swear in vile, bilious streams at Jesus and grab their weapons, anything at hand. In their hearts they know the futility of such efforts—but they are no longer capable of any other response. They must strike back. They must strike out at that which threatens the world they have built for themselves. They know well that it is all over. All that they had cherished is coming to its promised end and they flail violently in their rage.

> *Distressed and hungry, they will roam through the land; when they are famished, they will become enraged and, looking upward, will curse their king and their God. Then they will look toward the earth and see only distress and darkness and fearful gloom, and they will be thrust into utter darkness.*
>
> —Isaiah 8:21-22

Their resistance is hopeless and their fate is known. My comrades and I, the very people that God had described as *"a great nation,"* know well the exact order of the day:

> *"Look! An army is coming from the north; a great nation and many kings are being stirred up from the ends of the earth. They are armed with bows and spears; they are cruel and without mercy. They sound like the roaring sea as they ride on their horses; they come like men in battle formation to attack you, O Daughter of Babylon. The king of Babylon has heard reports about them, and his hands hang limp. Anguish has gripped him, pain like that of a woman in labor.*

Like a lion coming up from Jordan's thickets to a rich pastureland, I will chase Babylon from its land in an instant. Who is the chosen one I will appoint for this? Who is like me and who can challenge me? And what shepherd can stand against me?"

Therefore, hear what the LORD has planned against Babylon, what he has purposed against the land of the Babylonians: The young of the flock will be dragged away; he will completely destroy their pasture because of them. At the sound of Babylon's capture the earth will tremble; its cry will resound among the nations.

—Jeremiah 50:41-46 (emphasis added)

To those who know the Lord and call upon His Name, it is the greatest of days. It is the rescue of rescues. It is the fulfillment of all that they had hoped for, and more. But for those who had said *no*—said *no* a thousand times—it is the very depth of hell itself. It is the horror of knowing that for so long they had truly had a chance, but had said no. All that they have feared was true is undeniable now.

Chapter 16

The Fury of Battle

The armies of the Living God strike the elite forces of the evil one with the impact of a tidal wave on a reef. We sweep down behind our Savior and strike in a predetermined battle array in precisely the locations that had been ordained from the very beginning of time itself. By land and by air the impact of our engagement of the enemy is heard, seen, and felt by every person in every nation on earth. God had promised that everyone would know of the second coming of His Son and, to their horror or delight, every person now witnesses firsthand the vivid details of the battle.

My *Apache* formation sweeps in low over the desert. The silhouettes of our black gunships can be seen streaking in attack formation just above the sand dunes east of Basra. Without delay we press home the attack on our preordained primary targets.

We pop up over a huge dune and simultaneously dip the noses of our *Apaches* in perfect battle deployment. It is as if we have rehearsed our battle tactics a thousand times. I focus my attention on the rapidly developing battle topography while all the time my eyes are simultaneously locked on my battle commander, Jesus. My eternal capabilities are overwhelming. Every single bit of my attention is focused on Jesus, while at the very same time every single bit of my attention is focused on the battle before me. Jesus is not like some little computer icon in the corner of the screen of my life that I can just *click* on whenever I need a little *God-fix*. Quite to the contrary, Jesus is my literal *all in all,* my everything, my every moment. I still run with all of my might into the knowledge of the Holy, yet the battle still rages and my Redeemer and I are deeply involved in it together as close battle partners. My only desire, my overwhelming passion, is for Jesus, who is ever before me. Yet still I fly the *Apache* with Jesus in the seat next to me, like a copilot, like a friend, like the true director of my eternal life. The capacity to be simultaneously and exclusively involved in these two dramas at the same time had not even been imaginable during my life.

The battle rapidly reaches an indescribable level in its fury. The machine gunners on the enemy main battle tanks, and the commanders of the antiaircraft vehicles, straightaway respond to the new threat that has appeared above them. They had seen the attack unfolding from the very beginning. They had seen the flowing swarm of these mysterious black aircraft as it had streamed from the glowing clouds of God's glory above Jerusalem. And somehow they had known that we were coming for them.

The hail of gunfire that they now direct toward the *Apaches* is overwhelming. It lights up the early dawn like a massive fireworks display erroneously and prematurely set off by a carelessly thrown cigarette.

Our *Apaches* fly straight through the initial onslaught of the deadly barrage. The tough outer skin of the strange creature-machines appears to somehow absorb the bullets. They simply vanish as they hit the dull black outer skin with no damage to the *Apache* itself. I can, nonetheless, feel the impact of every shell making the gunship shudder, and hear the thumping of the ordinance against the *Apache* skin. It pounds like a huge subwoofer placed close to my chest. The staccato hammering impact of the 50-caliber rounds against the *Apache* and the dazzling array of explosions and brilliant flashes of light that burst by my windshield combine to pitch the battle frenzy to a furious level. Yet the fear that would have been a mandatory accompaniment of such an onslaught during my life is absent— for God sits in the seat next to me. My eyes are locked on Him. I remember how hard God had tried to tell me about this during my life, that fear is simply not possible when my eyes are focused on Jesus.

Now it is the turn of the blackened, hawk-like *Apaches*. I feel my hand squeeze down on one of the firing triggers built into the controller that wraps seamlessly around my right hand. I instinctively know which one to trigger as the enemy gun position comes into the gun-sight crosshairs that project automatically onto my retinas. My eyes target the weapons. Wherever I look, the weapons point. The flying beast and I are one. My Redeemer and I are one. Our purpose and intention are one. The taking of the fight to this enemy seems effortless.

The enemy rails angrily against us and against the remnant of the people of God that remains surrounded in the rocky hideout below. The fury of this enemy is unmatched by anything I had witnessed during my life. They continue to *"become enraged and ... curse their king and their God" (Isaiah 8:21)*. But now their fury is met by the fury of God. For Jesus now treads *"the winepress of the fury of the wrath of God" (Revelation 19:15)*. By God's merciful grace, that winepress is the combined forces of the armies of the Living God.

The *Apache* under my control bucks furiously as the weapons beneath its wings respond to my firing command. The large black beast recoils up and back from the reaction to the discharge of a mysteriously deafening weapon. Huge javelin-shaped flames of fire roar out from the array of beasts hovering above the crest of the dune as the entire *Apache* formation simultaneously unleashes its weapons. The roaring noise of the *Apache* wings is temporarily eclipsed by the cracking thunderclap that immediately precedes the appearance of the flaming spears of destruction. The impact of the luminescent darts upon their pre-assigned targets is sudden and devastating. The annihilation is complete. The targets are obliterated and the assailants, along with their deadly intentions, are scattered about the desert wasteland below.

> *Before them fire devours, behind them a flame blazes. Before them the land is like the garden of Eden, behind them, a desert waste—nothing escapes them. They have the appearance of horses; they gallop along like cavalry. With a noise like that of chariots they leap over the mountaintops, like a crackling fire consuming stubble, like a mighty army drawn up for battle.*
>
> —Joel 2:3-5

As if they are one, the Apaches perform a barrel roll escape maneuver that puts them immediately in position to fire again at the scraps of the rallying enemy below them. The Lord reigns over all as *"his chariots are like a whirlwind; he will bring down his anger with fury, and his rebuke with flames of fire" (Isaiah 66:15)*. At my command another volley of the devastating flaming darts pours forth from beneath the wings of my matte graphite-colored, armored gun ship. The entire group of ships immediately completes the attack by a seemingly well-practiced flare maneuver toward the enemy's right flank. I am now the most rightward hook on the end of the attack formation. As I come around for another attack, my Savior continues to encourage and instruct. He sings glorious battle songs of bravery and valor over me from His position seated beside me in the cockpit.

Suddenly, I notice a flurry of concentrated activity from an antiaircraft position to my right. The telltale signature of a surface-to-air missile appears above a puff of smoke from the fortified position. The shrill warning siren from my defense screen instantly blares a warning of the attack. But the siren is much deeper in tone than usual—*multiple threats*. It directs my attention back to the screen just in time to see not one, but six missiles being simultaneously tracked by the living machine that I am flying. The *Apache* convulses as it takes immediate evasive maneuvers. I am thrown to the left and then to the right as the ship patterns through an exaggerated attack escape protocol. The escape maneuvers occur too quickly for me to have triggered them. The living machine and I are a team. It detects the threats and responds before I can move the controls that enmesh my hands. I do not have to look at Jesus in my amazement, for I am continually looking at Jesus. There is no panic. There is no fear. There is only the self-assured feeling of complete security while sitting in the seat next to the Son of God.

And in this exact moment, my Savior decides to open my eyes to the fullness of the drama being played out below me. For now, as I strain against the g-forces to stare at the missiles from the left window of my arcing *Apache*, I can see that they seem somehow strangely different.

The missiles no longer have the smooth curving shape of the inanimate objects that a moment before had been hurtling toward my *Apache*. Instead, they have much more intricate detail. I can now see that they have small wings, almost bat-like, projecting from their sides. Their conical nose cones are quite irregular and seem somehow familiar. They appear to have faces, almost human, that are contorted in the most heinous of gargoyle grimaces. It is as if the missiles are somehow suffering from intense pain.

They streak toward my *Apache* with deadly precision—all six of them. As they draw closer, I can see why they are not fooled by the *Apache's* perfectly performed evasive maneuvers. Two demon eyes now peer from each missile. The missiles are alive. They are tracking me by direct sight.

All six close rapidly on their designated prey in a predetermined array designed to eliminate any possibility of escape. My gaze never leaves my Friend and Redeemer seated next to me. There is no panic. Jesus is, of course, all too aware of the surrounding fury of the battle. He simply says, "Do not be afraid of them." And that is it.

For with the same suddenness of the launch of the missile attack, the solution strikes with precision and finality. From six completely different directions, six intercepting angels streak suddenly into the fray. They have wings, just like in the visions that Isaiah and Ezekiel had described—and they move with incredible speed—like lightning. All brandish long glistening swords of white-hot fire. The swords are exaggeratedly long. They decimate the living-missile attack as they arc through the air. I hear the hard ringing metallic sound of metal hitting metal as the angels dispatch all six of the demon missiles within yards of my *Apache*. Their shattered body parts fly past my windows and flutter to the desert sand below, littering the battlefield like the contents of a peppermill.

My eyes are now fully open to the rest of the activity that is taking place on the battlefield below. Behind every single enemy tank or antiaircraft emplacement is a legion of demons! They are locked in battle with angels all across the battlefield. The combination of the combatants whom I had previously seen, and those who now become visible, make for indecipherable confusion on the battlefield below. The intensity and fury of the battle is overwhelming.

My eyes are also open to the true nature of the *aircraft* that I now guide effortlessly over the battlefield. There is a reason that I sensed that it was somehow alive. For as Jesus had chosen this moment to open my eyes to the very palpable spiritual battle that was furiously going on around me, so also did He open my eyes to the true nature of the *life* upon which—and in partnership with—I now fight this battle. The massive black flying beast that I pilot is a mighty warrior cherub! I partner in war with the mightiest of God's created beings, an *Apache cherub*.

> He parted the heavens and came down; *dark clouds were under his feet. He mounted the cherubim and flew; he soared on the wings of the wind.* He made darkness his canopy around him—the dark rain clouds of the sky. Out of the brightness of his presence *bolts of lightning blazed forth.* The LORD thundered from heaven; the voice of the Most High resounded. He *shot arrows* and scattered [the enemies], *bolts of lightning* and *routed them.*
> —2Samuel 22:10-15 (emphasis added)

I realize that I am not so much its pilot as I am its fellow combatant. We stand back-to-back in the fury of this battle as fellow warriors in the armies of the Living God. This is why it had responded to the missile threats before and quite independently of my command. This was why the weapons systems had been toggled before my finger had even moved. The *Apache* cherub takes his commands from the same Person who commands me. We combine to become a single weapon in the hand of the mighty Son of God.

With my eyes now wide open, my *Apache* formation immediately turns back toward the fortified missile battery that had fired on my ship. A different weapon than before is immediately—and without effort on my part—toggled and triggered. It simultaneously erupts from beneath each of the wings of each of the *Apache* cherubim in the reformed attack formation.

My mind is continually a chorus of the literal Word of God and I now live the words that I had only read before. For now huge hurtling explosive projectiles—that can only be described as hailstones—flash from beneath the main body of my living *Apache*. The words that had only been written before are now sung by a chorus of beautiful voices and fill my awareness completely. They emanate from the knowledge of the Holy that now fills this world around me and is seated on the seat beside me.

> *The earth trembled and quaked, and the foundations of the mountains shook; they trembled because he was angry. Smoke rose from his nostrils; consuming fire came from his mouth, burning coals blazed out of it. He parted the heavens and came down; dark clouds were under his feet.* *He mounted the cherubim and flew; he soared on the wings of the wind. He made darkness his covering, his canopy around him—the dark rain clouds of the sky. Out of the brightness of his presence clouds advanced, with hailstones and bolts of lightning. The* LORD *thundered from heaven; the voice of the Most High resounded. He shot his arrows and scattered [the enemies], great bolts of lightning and routed them.* *The valleys of the sea were exposed and the foundations of the earth laid bare at your rebuke, O* LORD*, at the blast of breath from your nostrils.*
>
> —Psalm 18:7-15 (emphasis added)

The effect of these light blue streaking projectiles immediately captures my attention. They appear to break into thousands of smaller blue projectiles several hundred yards above their targets. The spray of devastation that follows simply engulfs the missile launch platform. Only silence follows.

Chapter 17

Ground Forces and High-flying Fast Movers

As my formation pulls up from the devastation of the missile platform, I can see the advancing columns of the ground forces of the armies of the Living God. I can now see my sons, William, Ryan, and Michael, marching in the columns of foot soldiers. They brandish swords as their only weapons. The swords appear similar to those wielded by the angels that had attacked the surface-to-air missiles. They seem very long to me. Their exaggerated length almost makes them a caricature of swords I had seen during my life. Their blades glow with the fire of God.

From my position above the battlefield, I can see the foot soldiers as their columns storm over the enemy emplacements below. Fierce hand-to-hand combat results. I remember the fear that I would have had in a similar situation during my sons' lives. But there is no fear now. Their eternal destinies are written on the hands of Almighty God now, just as they had been during their lives. Only now it is so different. Now I know directly and immediately the love and faithfulness of God. The same opportunity to know God personally in this manner had been available during my life. How I wish that I had taken advantage of it then. My vision had been so clouded by my focus on myself and on the *reality* projected by the world, rather than on God. Now, since Jesus never leaves my vision, there simply is no fear for my sons as they wade into the enemy forces with their swords swinging widely. I am continually and completely reassured.

The lethal effectiveness of their weapons as they swing them in great arcs through the middle of the enemy troops is readily apparent. The enemy soldiers keep firing their machine guns at the advancing columns and react with utter disbelief at the complete ineffectiveness of the bullets that spray forth from their weapons. They simply have no effect on the advancing troops. Nor do the fiery blasts from their grenades and mortar shells have the expected effect.

> *When you walk through the fire, you will not be burned; the flames will not set you ablaze.*

—Isaiah 43:2

The foot soldiers of the armies of the Living God simply march straight through the onslaught.

> *They all march in line, not swerving from their course. They do not jostle each other; each marches straight ahead. They plunge through defenses without breaking ranks.*
>
> —Joel 2:7-8

I can see why the enemy warriors' weapons are so completely ineffective. Now I can see the angels of God flashing back and forth, deflecting projectiles and shielding the individual warriors as they advance. They move with the immediacy of lightning. When the warriors of God clash against the enemy soldiers in full hand-to-hand combat, the angels of God hurl themselves against the demons that are supporting the enemy soldiers. It is just as it had been during our lives, except that now we can actually see the intensity of the angels' protective measures. Where the battle is most intense, the individual combatants blend together into a mass of writhing warriors with arms extending and swords flashing. I can hardly tell the individuals apart where the battle lines are enjoined.

The resistance of the dark forces is pointless as the swinging swords of the advancing armies of the Living God wreak steady devastation upon the enemy before them.

> *"Assyria will fall by a sword that is not of man; a sword, not of mortals, will devour them. They will flee before the sword and their young men will be put to forced labor. Their stronghold will fall because of terror; at sight of the battle standard their commanders will panic," declares the LORD, whose fire is in Zion, whose furnace is in Jerusalem.*
>
> —Isaiah 31:8-9

The panic of the remaining enemy soldiers, which results from the seeming invincibility of the holy warriors who swarm through their encampment, does not quench their rage. Those who do not run before the advancing army of God turn with fury on their faces and throw themselves zealously—utterly chaotic in their panic—against the foot soldiers and their blazing swords. Their destruction is complete.

Charging cavalry, flashing swords and glittering spears! Many casualties, piles of dead, bodies without number, people stumbling over the corpses—

—Nahum 3:3

The childhood dreams of every one of God's foot soldiers are magnificently complete in the battle below. Their hearts had been made for this day—and God had told them precisely this throughout their lives. I could not have known that my sons' wild swinging of wooden swords against imaginary backyard foes had been a twinkling premonition of the magnificent battle that unfolds now in the desert hills below me.

My brother Jonathan, who had often stared at the skulking form of an F-14 Tomcat Navy fighter on a carrier deck and wondered why his attention was repeatedly drawn back to it, now knows well the meaning of the dreams that had pleasantly intruded on his adult life. For his dream had always been to streak low and fast across the hills "like a bat out of hell" in the front seat of an F-14. He had often said that he couldn't wait to get to heaven because he "just knew" that there would be F-14's there for him to fly. Jonathan had no idea what God had in store for him. For now he is seated in the cockpit of one of the glistening *fast movers* that streak overhead. And his *back seat* copilot is the Lord God of Hosts and the King of kings, Jesus.

The acrobatic flight of these strangely familiar aircraft bears a marked resemblance to that of a red-tailed hawk in predatory attack. They are fierce in appearance, and despite their silver metallic appearance—like sinuous, flowing aluminum—they appear very much alive like the gunship that I am flying. Unlike the *Apaches*, however, these birds of prey do not fly in groups. They appear to be a swarm of individual aircraft continually engaging the enemy ground targets, all controlled by the only Controller now. There are no organized formations. Each has no need for a wingman, because the Lord of lords has their wing. They move in perfect coordination despite acting as individually separate attack elements.

The weapons they carry are similar to the *Apaches*, more hailstones and lightning. Bright blue fireballs sweep out in dazzling sparkling array from beneath their wings. Their targeting capabilities are like those of the *Apaches* with lethal accuracy and unrivaled domination of the skies over the battlefield. I cannot help but be amazed at the totality of the destruction.

The sword of the LORD is bathed in blood...For the LORD has a sacrifice in Bozrah and a great slaughter in Edom.

—Isaiah 34:6

For the LORD has a day of vengeance, a year of retribution, to uphold Zion's cause. Edom's streams will be turned into pitch, her dust into burning sulfur; her land will become blazing pitch! It will not be quenched night and day; its smoke will rise forever. From generation to generation it will lie desolate; no one will ever pass through it again.

—Isaiah 34:8-10

That part of the antichrist's army that had sought the destruction of the hiding Jewish remnant is itself now destroyed.

Were you angry with the rivers, O LORD? Was your wrath against the streams? Did you rage against the sea <u>when you rode with your horses and your victorious chariots? You uncovered your bow, you called for many arrows.</u> Selah You split the earth with rivers; the mountains saw you and writhed. Torrents of water swept by; the deep roared and lifted its waves on high.

Sun and moon stood still in the heavens <u>at the glint of your flying arrows</u>, <u>at the lightning of your flashing spear</u>. In wrath you strode through the earth and in anger <u>you threshed the nations</u>. <u>You came out to deliver your people</u>, to save your anointed one. You crushed the leader of the land of wickedness, you stripped him from head to foot. Selah. With his own spear you pierced his head <u>when his warriors stormed out to scatter us, gloating as though about to devour the wretched who were in hiding</u>. You trampled the sea with your horses, churning the great waters.

—Habakkuk 3:8-15 (emphasis added)

The victory belongs to Jesus. This is His day. It is the day of the Lord that had been spoken of for centuries and it is God's empowered warriors who rule this day. The birds that had been called by the Word of the Lord now circle overhead, and the scavenging beasts gather already on the fringes of the battlefield.

This is what the Sovereign LORD says: "'With a great throng of people I will cast my net over you, and they will haul you up in my net. I will throw you on the land and hurl you on the open field. I will let all the birds of the air settle on you and all the beasts of the earth gorge themselves on you. I will spread your flesh on the mountains and fill the valleys with your remains. I will drench the land with your flowing blood all the way to the mountains, and the ravines will be filled with your flesh.

—Ezekiel 32:3-6

Chapter 18

The Battle for Jerusalem

> *I will gather all the nations to Jerusalem to fight against it; the city will be captured, the houses ransacked, and the women raped. Half of the city will go into exile, but the rest of the people will not be taken from the city. Then the LORD will go out and fight against those nations, as he fights in the day of battle.*
>
> *On that day his feet will stand on the Mount of Olives, east of Jerusalem, and the Mount of Olives will be split in two from east to west, forming a great valley, with half of the mountain moving north and half moving south. You will flee by my mountain valley, for it will extend to Azel. You will flee as you fled from the earthquake in the days of Uzziah king of Judah. Then the LORD my God will come, and all the holy ones with him.*
>
> —Zechariah 14:2-5 (emphasis added)

As quickly as it had begun, the battle at Basra is over. The Jewish remnant that had hidden there during the reign of the antichrist—after his defiling of the temple—is rescued. Not a single one of *the chosen* has been lost. As the forces of evil had surrounded them, they had cried out to the Lord. It had occurred precisely as Jesus had foretold. It had occurred exactly as recorded in the Gospel of Matthew.

> *"O Jerusalem, Jerusalem, you who kill the prophets and stone those sent to you, how often I have longed to gather your children together, as a hen gathers her chicks under her wings, but you were not willing. Look, your house is left to you desolate.*
>
> *For I tell you, you will not see me again until you say, 'Blessed is he who comes in the name of the Lord.'"*
>
> —Matthew 23:37-39 (emphasis added)

The forces of evil surrounding the Jews at Basra had raged in their unquenchable anger against the swarming armies of the Living God—until every last one of them had been destroyed.

Now, quite suddenly, there is silence on the battlefield. The army of the redeemed, ever aware of the written Word, knows well that this was only a small portion of the army of the antichrist. The rest of his troops are amassing elsewhere.

> *Then the dragon was enraged at the woman and went off to make war against the rest of her offspring—those who obey God's commandments and hold to the testimony of Jesus.*
>
> —Revelation 12:17

Now, all eyes are fixed on the Lamb of God. He stands before His entire army, His blood-spattered robes visible to every eye. There is silence. Then, with knowing intent, He turns. His eyes face west toward Jerusalem. The armies of the Living God, all of the foot soldiers, the main battle tank commanders, the *Apache* drivers, the *fast-mover* pilots—all of us—turn as one toward Jerusalem.

For a cry comes up from Jerusalem, from Ariel. Now we all hear it as He had first heard it. It is a mournful wail of suffering and repentance, a cry unto God.

> *"And I will pour out on the house of David and the inhabitants of Jerusalem a spirit of grace and supplication. They will look on me, the one they have pierced, and they will mourn for him as one mourns for an only child, and grieve bitterly for him as one grieves for a firstborn son.*
>
> —Zechariah 12:10

It is the cry that waits restrained in every heart, yearning for its long-awaited unleashing. This is the cry that is smothered over by pride and sin. And it is the cry that is unleashed when men and women acknowledge the complete bankruptcy of their hearts and minds and souls in that moment when they fully realize the awesome glory of their Maker. It is the cry that can come only from a heart completely humbled in *"grace and supplication"* before the God of All. I had not known until now that the entire heavenly host had heard the very same cry on the most important day of *my* life. For on that day I had fully realized the depth to which I had sunk so long ago and had finally surrendered my heart to the King of kings.

The cry from His people in Jerusalem is like beautiful music in Jesus' ears, and He smiles. He smiles on the seat next to me. He smiles standing next to my foot-soldier sons. He smiles in the back seat of my brother Jonathan's sleek silver *fast-mover*.

> *O people of Zion, who live in Jerusalem, you will weep no more. How gracious he will be when you cry for help!* <u>*As soon as he hears, he will answer you.*</u>
>
> —Isaiah 30:19 (emphasis added)

Jesus smiles as He sits before us on His magnificent and impatient white stallion. All of us praise the glory of His perfect Holiness, His perfect faithfulness, His perfect infinite mercy, and His compassion—which always pour forth when the hearts of men turn from their sinful ways. These attributes of the very nature of Jesus, fully God and fully man, mandate only one response to the mournful cry. He is capable of nothing less.

> *And everyone who calls on the name of the LORD <u>will be saved</u>; for on Mount Zion and in Jerusalem there will be deliverance, as the LORD has said, among the survivors whom the LORD calls.*
>
> —Joel 2:32 (emphasis added)

There is no uncertainty in His answer to their cry. The Living Word once again becomes the fulfillment of all that is the written Word:

> *"Shout and be glad, O Daughter of Zion. <u>For I am coming</u>, and I will live among you," declares the LORD.*
>
> —Zechariah 2:10 (emphasis added)

All of the armies of the Living God cry out in unison toward Jerusalem:

> *... say to those with fearful hearts, "Be strong, do not fear; your God will come, he will come with vengeance; with divine retribution he will come to save you."*
>
> —Isaiah 35:4

Jesus immediately moves in symphony with all of creation toward the city that He cherishes, toward the people who now cry out, toward the temple that waits for the promised liberation. It is a scene that is known to all of us from the declarations of the prophets. It has waited patiently in every heart in eager anticipation of its glorious fulfillment.

> *The LORD has made proclamation to the ends of the earth: "Say to the Daughter of Zion, 'See, your Savior comes! See, his reward is with him, and his recompense accompanies him.'" They will be called the Holy People, the Redeemed of the LORD; and you will be called Sought After, the City No Longer Deserted.*

> *Who is this coming from Edom, from Bozrah, with his garments stained crimson? Who is this, robed in splendor, striding forward in the greatness of his strength? "It is I, speaking in righteousness, mighty to save."*

> *Why are your garments red, like those of one treading the winepress?*

> *"I have trodden the winepress alone; from the nations no one was with me. I trampled them in my anger and trod them down in my wrath; their blood spattered my garments, and I stained all my clothing.*

> *For the day of vengeance was in my heart, and the year of my redemption has come. I looked, but there was no one to help, I was appalled that no one gave support; so my own arm worked salvation for me, and my own wrath sustained me.*
> —Isaiah 62:11-12; 63:1-5 (emphasis added)

Each and every member of the army of the redeemed remembers well how Jesus had answered on the day that each of us had cried out to Him. Each of us acted as individuals then and every one of our circumstances was unique. But His answer is always the same, always true to His compassion and mercy. He had answered then as He answers Jerusalem now, with the victory of the cross as His strength and righteousness. Each of us in the very depth of our individual corruption had reached up, and the saving Right Arm of Almighty God had reached down. We had been ushered into the kingdom of God forever. A spontaneous cry now rises up in the throats of all who move as one under the banner of the Lamb.

> *Praise be to the LORD, for he has heard my cry for mercy. The LORD is my strength and my shield; my heart trusts in him, and I am helped. My heart leaps for joy and I will give thanks to him in song.*

—Psalm 28:6-7

His glory is the all-encompassing, wholehearted joy of our hearts. Our eyes are fixed upon Him and Him alone. His will is our only thought and our only passion. We know the power of the Word as it had been proclaimed:

> *See, the Name of the LORD comes from afar, with burning anger and dense clouds of smoke; his lips are full of wrath, and his tongue is a consuming fire. His breath is like a rushing torrent, rising up to the neck. He shakes the nations in the sieve of destruction; he places in the jaws of the peoples a bit that leads them astray. And you will sing as on the night you celebrate a holy festival; your hearts will rejoice as when people go up with flutes to the mountain of the LORD, to the Rock of Israel. The LORD will cause men to hear his majestic voice and will make them see his arm coming down with raging anger and consuming fire, with cloudburst, thunderstorm and hail.*
> —Isaiah 30:27-30

Without thought, I swing my gunship around, as do all of those who accompany me. There is no feeling of fatigue. There is only glorious anticipation of the victory long predicted. There is only anticipation of the recapture of the city that God cherishes above all others, the city that will be the center of His rule, the city of the throne of His servant David. This is the victory that the Son of the Living God had anticipated, promised, and won on the cross of Calvary. It had been this joy of this anticipated victory—in the accompaniment of those redeemed—that had kept Him on the cross. Now He rides toward the City of David in magnificent fulfillment of the written Word.

As we near Jerusalem we can see the forces of the evil one that surround the ancient city in a modern-day siege. They are under the guidance of the antichrist. He raged against the Jewish population that had dared to take back their city. Isaiah's words are so accurate that it is as if the prophet had choreographed every move. For in the seemingly independent assault of the armies of the antichrist on Jerusalem, they had in fact become instruments of God.

> *Woe to you, Ariel, Ariel, the city where David settled! Add year to year and let your cycle of festivals go on. Yet I will besiege Ariel; she will mourn and lament, she will be to me like an altar hearth. I will encamp against you all around; I will encircle you with towers and set up my siege works against you.*

Brought low, you will speak from the ground; your speech will mumble out of the dust. Your voice will come ghostlike from the earth; out of the dust your speech will whisper.
—Isaiah 29:1-4 (emphasis added)

It is the whisper of the remnant that we hear. A low mournful whisper that will change to glorious, shouted praise as the rest of the Scripture is fulfilled.

But your many enemies will become like fine dust, the ruthless hordes like blown chaff. Suddenly, in an instant, the LORD Almighty will come with thunder and earthquake and great noise, with windstorm and tempest and flames of a devouring fire.

Then the hordes of all the nations that fight against Ariel, that attack her and her fortress and besiege her, will be as it is with a dream, with a vision in the night—as when a hungry man dreams that he is eating, but he awakens, and his hunger remains; as when a thirsty man dreams that he is drinking, but he awakens faint, with his thirst unquenched. So will it be with the hordes of all the nations that fight against Mount Zion.
—Isaiah 29:5-8 (emphasis added)

The fate of the besieging armies has already been spelled out in detail. It cannot be stated more clearly than Isaiah has already proclaimed. Once again the written Word's fulfillment is found totally in the Living Word. For now Jesus, the conquering King of kings, leads the armies of the Living God toward the beleaguered city. The infantry, armored cavalry, and the low-flying *Apache* gunships move rapidly into the assault positions that had been rehearsed since the beginning in the eternal plan that now fills our minds and empowers our hearts. For the resolute purpose of Jesus, in His role as *the Avenger of Blood*, is known by all of us by the Word of God written on our hearts.

On that day I will set out to destroy all the nations that attack Jerusalem.
—Zechariah 12:9

The onslaught of the armies of the Lord is not lost on the entrenched armies of the antichrist. They had been confident of victory after laying siege to Jerusalem.

Their response to the vast array of troops and weaponry now arrayed before them is predictable because, in fact, it was predicted.

At the sight of them, nations are in anguish; every face turns pale.

—Joel 2:6

The reaction of the faithful in Jerusalem is understandably different. They realize their redemption is at hand, that the only One who can help them now has indeed heard their cry for help. The hopeless situation is now joyous in hope. They see the advancing forces of God's redemption army.

How beautiful on the mountains are the feet of those who bring good news, who proclaim peace, who bring good tidings, who proclaim salvation, who say to Zion, "Your God reigns!"

Listen! Your watchmen lift up their voices; together they shout for joy. When the LORD returns to Zion, they will see it with their own eyes. Burst into songs of joy together, you ruins of Jerusalem, for the LORD has comforted his people, he has redeemed Jerusalem.

The LORD will lay bare his holy arm in the sight of all the nations, and all the ends of the earth will see the salvation of our God.

Depart, depart, go out from there! Touch no unclean thing! Come out from it and be pure, you who carry the vessels of the LORD. But you will not leave in haste or go in flight; for the LORD will go before you, the God of Israel will be your rear guard.

—Isaiah 52:7-12

The combined forces of the armies of the Living God throw themselves against the enemy. The confident dark army had captured part of the city and now surrounded the rest. God's foot soldiers move rapidly, systematically, as one. Their purpose is never in doubt.

The shields of his soldiers are red; the warriors are clad in scarlet. The metal on the chariots flashes on the day they are made ready; the spears of pine are brandished. The chariots storm through the streets, rushing back and forth through the squares. They look like flaming torches; they dart about like lightning.

—Nahum 2:3-4 (emphasis added)

Jesus now sings victory psalms above each of them in the climactic assault. Their roles are clear and the outcome is known from the beginning.

> *They charge like warriors; they scale walls like soldiers. They all march in line, not swerving from their course. They do not jostle each other; each marches straight ahead. They plunge through defenses without breaking ranks. They rush upon the city; they run along the wall. They climb into the houses; like thieves they enter through the windows. Before them the earth shakes, the sky trembles, the sun and moon are darkened, and the stars no longer shine.*
>
> —Joel 2:7-10

The ominously pounding sound of my black beast-of-prey hammers the ears of the besieging army as I fly low over the city. The whole company of low-slung *Apaches* descends into the city like a plague of locusts. Our assignment is tactical ground support for the foot soldiers of God who are taking the fight directly to the enemy. The thunderous sound of the whirling wings of our *Apaches* and the roar from the fast movers overhead are, indeed, the *"great noise, with windstorm and tempest" (Isaiah 29:6)* that had been proclaimed in the Word of God.

Out of the corner of my eye, and yet somehow fully in my view, I can see the *fast-movers* sweeping in from on high. They also fly in support of the ground invasion of the city. I can see my brother, Jonathan. God is glorifying him in his sleek *fast-mover*. They sweep in with their awesome weapons. The exact precision of the individually targeted projectiles is made possible only by the hand of God as He directs His streaking angels in their assistance of the warriors of the redeemed. Together they pour the *"flames of a devouring fire"* that the prophet Isaiah had promised (Isaiah 29:6), effectively and precisely upon the forces opposing the people of Jerusalem. The effect of these devastating weapons of divine wrath upon the individual enemy soldiers is unlike anything ever visited upon an earthly battlefield.

The words of the prophets, the words of all who are recorded in the Holy Word of God, are always there before us. They go before us into the fight like battle standards from above. For all that had been seemingly separate before is now unified. We are one with the written Word, which by its revealed nature is *of* the Living Word. For the written Word of God is continually visible in our minds and it is one with the Living Son who accompanies, encourages, and praises us. It is the very expression of the Living God. It speaks to us all of the victory that is ours in our Commander, Jesus. It is ever present, ever guiding, and ever true.

During my life I had, by my sinful focus on myself, placed limits upon the impact of the written Word of God. It had been a reference that I had read and feebly tried to keep in my mind only when *I* thought I *needed* it. Now I realize that I always *need* it and it is simply always there—as is the Son, its source and its realization. It is all. It is everything. It is eternal and ever present. It teaches, guides, instructs, and fulfills. It is a continual symphony declaring to all the everlasting glory of the One and Only.

Now the written Word speaks specifically of the Jewish remnant in the city. Overwhelmed at the sight of the redemption that is crashing down upon them, the remnant rises up as one against the armies of evil that had laid siege to their city.

> *In that day the LORD Almighty will be a glorious crown, a beautiful wreath for the remnant of his people. He will be a spirit of justice to him who sits in judgment, <u>a source of strength to those who turn back the battle at the gate.</u>*
>
> —Isaiah 28:5-6 (emphasis added)

My formation and I swing our *Apaches* in front of the advancing army of God and lay down the deafening *"devouring fire"* that is the very wrath of the Living God. The enemy troops, so entirely engulfed in their raging blindness, now hurl themselves against the advancing army just as the enemy had at Basra. Mass terror and confusion reign among them on the battlefield and their weapons become weapons in the hand of God.

> *On that day men will be stricken by the LORD with great panic. Each man will seize the hand of another, and they will attack each other.*
>
> —Zechariah 14:13

Into this confusion the war machines of the armies of God continue to pour devastation. Its effects are sudden and complete. The bodies of the besieging forces of the antichrist lay strewn along every road and in every entrenchment that had been constructed in anticipation of this battle for the City of God. The saturation of their deception leaves them all, to the very last man, enraged beyond all sense. Just as in Basra, the besiegers of Jerusalem fight madly, uncontrollably, and without remorse until every last one of them lays slain. For their sin-blinded rage overflows from their eternally unrepentant hearts, assuring once again that there are no survivors.

> *And you will again see the distinction between the righteous and the wicked, between those who serve God and those who do not. "Surely the day is coming; it will burn like a furnace. <u>All the arrogant and every evildoer will be stubble,</u> and that day that is coming <u>will set them on fire,"</u> says the LORD Almighty. <u>"Not a root or a branch will be left to them</u>.*

> *But for you who revere my name, the sun of righteousness will rise with healing in its wings. And you will go out and leap like calves released from the stall.*

> *Then you will <u>trample down the wicked; they will be ashes under the soles of your feet on the day when I do these things,"</u> says the LORD Almighty.*
>
> —Malachi 3:18-4:3 (emphasis added)

For countless centuries these battles have always been fought at two levels, the physical and the spiritual. These final battles, however, are different. For somehow the two battlefields, the warfare of the flesh and the spiritual warfare, the visible and the invisible, are united. I can now see the drama of the conquest of God's mighty warrior angels. They fight in full support of the battle that we, the redeemed, now wage against the army of the antichrist. Only the reckless fanaticism of the demons that fight behind and empower them surpasses that of the soldiers of the antichrist.

God's warrior angels are taking the fight to them, as they have for every moment of every day since the dawn of man. Until now, the ferocity of this *spiritual* battle had been kept behind the scenes, always just out of the view of the saints. The spiritual warfare that is now fully revealed is furious as the fanatical demons throw themselves against the swinging swords of the angelic host. I am astonished at the intensity of this previously hidden holocaust. How naïve I had been to this warfare during my life.

But, this is *"the day of the LORD."* This is the day of the humble Savior who is also the Avenger of blood.

The Spirit of the Sovereign LORD is on me, because the LORD has anointed me to preach good news to the poor. He has sent me to bind up the brokenhearted, to proclaim freedom for the captives and release from darkness for the prisoners, to proclaim the year of the LORD'S favor and <u>the day of vengeance of our God</u>, to comfort all who mourn, and provide for those who grieve in Zion—to bestow on them a crown of beauty instead of ashes, the oil of gladness instead of mourning, and a garment of praise instead of a spirit of despair. They will be called oaks of righteousness, a planting of the LORD for the display of his splendor.

—Isaiah 61:1-3 (emphasis added)

The victory of Jesus over the forces of evil is complete. As the besieging armies of the antichrist are defeated, so also are the legions of Satan that accompany them. The Word of the Lord is triumphant:

On that day they will say to Jerusalem, "Do not fear, O Zion; do not let your hands hang limp. The LORD your God is with you, he is mighty to save. He will take great delight in you, he will quiet you with his love, he will rejoice over you with singing."

—Zephaniah 3:16-17

Chapter 19

Armageddon

"The great day of the LORD is near—near and coming quickly. Listen! The cry on the day of the LORD will be bitter, the shouting of the warrior there. That day will be a day of wrath, a day of distress and anguish, a day of trouble and ruin, a day of darkness and gloom, a day of clouds and blackness, a day of trumpet and battle cry against the fortified cities and against the corner towers.

I will bring distress on the people and they will walk like blind men, because they have sinned against the LORD. Their blood will be poured out like dust and their entrails like filth. Neither their silver nor their gold will be able to save them on the day of the LORD's wrath. In the fire of his jealousy the whole world will be consumed, for he will make a sudden end of all who live in the earth."
—Zephaniah 1:14-18

"Therefore wait for me," declares the LORD, "for the day I will stand up to testify. I have decided to assemble the nations, to gather the kingdoms and to pour out my wrath on them—all my fierce anger. The whole world will be consumed by the fire of my jealous anger."
—Zephaniah 3:8

Just as at Basra, the battle against the armies of the antichrist that had been deployed against Jerusalem ends as abruptly as it had begun. Nevertheless, we know that we are not finished. Our work is not complete. For Jesus continues to tell us our future by recounting the written Word to each of us personally.

Then I saw three evil spirits that looked like frogs; they came out of the mouth of the dragon, out of the mouth of the beast and out of the mouth of the false prophet. They are spirits of demons performing miraculous signs, and they go out to the kings of the whole world, to gather them for the battle on the great day of God Almighty.
—Revelation 16:13-14 (emphasis added)

Then they gathered the kings together to the place that in Hebrew is called Armageddon.

—Revelation 16:16

We have defeated the elite guard units of the army of the antichrist that had attacked the Jewish remnant at Basra and Jerusalem. But as we had been fighting in Basra and in Jerusalem, the antichrist had been notably absent. He had been busy elsewhere. From the very first—from the moment of the appearance of Jesus to every nation on earth—he had remained hidden from sight. He had more on his mind than the remnant at Basra and the siege of Jerusalem. They were not the focus of his grand plan. In fact, in his mind Basra and Jerusalem were sideshows. They had served their purpose. They had delayed the armies of the Living God long enough for the antichrist to prepare for the real showdown. His forces had been at a numerical disadvantage to this point. This would be corrected in the final confrontation. The antichrist was betting everything on his final play.

The leaders of the nations of the earth had reacted immediately, wholeheartedly, and massively to his call for their armies. In their fear, they had responded unconditionally to the call of the antichrist to gather *"together to make war against the rider on the horse and his army" (Revelation 19:19)*. While the armies of the Living God had been fighting the battles at Basra and for Jerusalem, the beast had been gathering the nations—on the plains of *Armageddon*.

Proclaim this among the nations: Prepare for war! Rouse the warriors! Let all the fighting men draw near and attack. Beat your plowshares into swords and your pruning hooks into spears. Let the weakling say, 'I am strong!' Come quickly, all you nations from every side, and assemble there. Bring down your warriors, O LORD!

—Joel 3:9-11

The leaders of the nations of the Earth and their armies now stand massed together with the beast as their leader. Together they comprise the single largest and most powerful fighting force that has ever been gathered in one place—in all of history.

Let them all come together and take their stand; they will be brought down to terror and infamy.

—Isaiah 44:11

None of this surprises Jesus. His response catches us off guard—although it really shouldn't. He responds to the most daunting threat that the world has to offer by singing victory songs to each of us. He praises us for the exploits of the day. And He speaks to each of us of a job not yet finished. As He speaks face-to-face to me, He also speaks to each and every one of the redeemed. At the same time, He slowly turns on His white horse before us all.

And then he is off.

Jesus, like the perfection of every hero ever depicted in any of the great adventure movies, thunders down the streets of Jerusalem with elbows flying and his hair blown back in the wind. He is heading toward the battlefield of old called *Armageddon*. All of the armies of the Living God turn in formation and follow Him, some on foot, some in battle tanks, some in high-flying *fast-movers* of many different kinds, and my comrades and I in our *Apaches*.

A truly massive army is deployed against us on the plain of Armageddon. And yet, there is no fear. Quite to the contrary, there is only the excited anticipation of this final battle on the battlefield that has been spoken of for centuries. The battle song that we all now sing is the only sound that rises above the thunderous roar of the determined movement of the armies of the Living God.

> *Great is our Lord and mighty in power; his understanding has no limit. The LORD sustains the humble but casts the wicked to the ground.*
>
> —Psalm 147:5-6

> *His pleasure is not in the strength of the horse, nor his delight in the legs of a man; the LORD delights in those who fear him, who put their hope in his unfailing love.*
>
> —Psalm 147:10-11

> *The LORD reigns, let the nations tremble; he sits enthroned between the cherubim, let the earth shake. Great is the LORD in Zion; he is exalted over all the nations. Let them praise your great and awesome name—he is holy. The King is mighty, he loves justice—you have established equity; in Jacob you have done what is just and right. Exalt the LORD our God and worship at his footstool; he is holy.*
>
> —Psalm 99:1-5

Jesus reins-in his sweating white battle charger as He crests the top of a hill overlooking the massive enemy armies gathered on the plains below. We deploy immediately behind Him in a huge crescent-shaped semicircle around the massed troops. There we stop. All eyes look to the Glorious One as He sits silently upon His white horse before the armies that rage in their anger and rebellion in the valley below.

The question in my heart—and in the hearts of all of the redeemed—is immediately answered by Jesus. There by our sides He speaks personally to each of us:

"Not this one. This one is mine."

> *"Sit at my right hand until I make your enemies a footstool for your feet."*
>
> —Psalm 110:1

The sound of His words, echoing across the valley, is just loud enough that every ear hears nothing else but the intent of the Rider before them. The enraged armies of evil immediately retort from the bilious cores of their sin-darkened hearts. Their response truly measures the depth of their blindness and speaks only of the evil that rules their hearts:

> *"Who is like the beast? Who can make war against him?"*
>
> —Revelation 13:4

All of the armies of the redeemed immediately shout *"like the roar of a great multitude"* (Revelation 19:1) in praise of the King of kings. As that great shout of praise arises from every mouth, Jesus, beside each of them, recounts the words written so long ago:

> *Let the nations be roused; let them advance into the Valley of Jehoshaphat, for there I will sit to judge all the nations on every side. Swing the sickle, for the harvest is ripe. Come, trample the grapes, for the winepress is full and the vats overflow—so great is their wickedness.*
>
> *Multitudes, multitudes in the valley of decision! For the day of the LORD is near in the valley of decision. The sun and moon will be darkened, and the stars no longer shine. The LORD will roar from*

Zion and thunder from Jerusalem; the earth and the sky will tremble. But the LORD will be a refuge for his people, a stronghold for the people of Israel.

—Joel 3:12-16

As He speaks these words beside each of us, fire simultaneously erupts from the Rider Who sits upon the great white steed. Jesus never leaves my side. He never leaves any of us. Yet He also now sits transfigured before us on His horse and before the amassed enemy armies. Such is the universe and such are the dimensions in which we will spend eternity with Jesus. For as Jesus, beside each and every one of us, whispers these words of the prophet Joel, streams of blazing white fire—pure light, raw energy—simultaneously pour forth from the lips of He who speaks these words, from the mouth of the transfigured Christ. Not a separate Christ, for He is somehow *One*, in complete unity, as He also simultaneously interacts with every individual of the army of the redeemed.

His head and hair were white like wool, as white as snow, and his eyes were like blazing fire. His feet were like bronze glowing in a furnace, and his voice was like the sound of rushing waters. In his right hand he held seven stars, and out of his mouth came a sharp double-edged sword. His face was like the sun shining in all its brilliance.

—Revelation 1:14-16

Individual streams of fire detonate forth with a deafening thunderous crack and simultaneously hit every single soldier arrayed before the Lord of lords and King of kings. The streams of liquid lightning hit each one of the million mercenaries individually as if this spectacular onslaught had been generated for that soldier alone. Jesus, beside each of the redeemed, personally reminds us that the effects of His winnowing fire on each of the soldiers who stand defiantly against the Most Holy had been told to them long ago.

This is the plague with which the LORD will strike all the nations that fought against Jerusalem: Their flesh will rot while they are still standing on their feet, their eyes will rot in their sockets, and their tongues will rot in their mouths.

—Zechariah 14:12

Before our eyes, every single raging warrior—who the moment before had been consumed in their hatred of the Son of the Living God—literally decomposes under the intensity of the energy that bursts forth from Jesus. Their eyes and tongues and skin simply melt as the flame consumes them.

> *He will not escape the darkness; a flame will wither his shoots, and the breath of God's mouth will carry him away.*
>
> —Job 15:30

I am momentarily staggered by the dazzling spectacle that has exploded before me. I immediately remember how often I had wondered about the mysterious Biblical description of *the sword* emanating from the mouth of the Lamb of God.

> *The rest of them were killed with the sword that came out of the mouth of the rider on the horse...*
>
> —Revelation 19:21

I had always been taught that the *"sword"* represented the Word of God in allegorical form—that it is just a type or a symbol for the written Word of God. But in this final climactic scene from this battle of battles, there comes a much deeper understanding. The sword of God's pure light represents so much more. This sword of justice and vengeance is an inseparable attribute of the written Word of God and the Living Word of God. It is, in them, the very expression of God to man. The sword now speaks volumes to every man of the infinite purity and holiness of the Mighty God. Its pure energy pouring forth from the mouth of God before our eyes is the most absolute expression of the glory, majesty, righteousness, and holiness of the Living God. It now finishes what, to that point, had been so incomplete. It rights all wrongs and wipes evil—all that is not holy—from the face of God's created Earth in one final bold stroke of God's awesome prophetic pen. It, the sword, is the completion that is demanded by the very nature of the Only Holy One. This is the literal fulfillment of the words that Jesus last spoke upon the cross of His sacrifice, the cross of His ultimate victory:

> *"Tetelesti!"—It is finished.*
>
> —John 19:30

The antichrist and everyone who stands with him, along with every demon that stands behind Satan, all fall together on the field of Armageddon.

> *Then I saw the beast and the kings of the earth and their armies gathered together to make war against the rider on the horse and his army. But the beast was captured, and with him the false prophet who*

had performed the miraculous signs on his behalf. With these signs he had deluded those who had received the mark of the beast and worshiped his image. The two of them were thrown alive into the fiery lake of burning sulfur. The rest of them were killed with the sword that came out of the mouth of the rider on the horse, and all the birds gorged themselves on their flesh.

—Revelation 19:19-21

As the last enemy soldier falls into the ashes of the Armageddon battlefield, so also rises Michael, God's mighty archangel. It is Michael, by the power of the Lamb, who will complete the victory. It is left to him to vanquish Satan. Jesus turns to His mighty angel, who stands ever ready beside Him, and simply says,

"Go get him."

For Jesus Himself will not soil His majesty and glory by dealing with this Satan, this underling, this deceiver, this *created*, this impostor of the glory of God.

And I saw an angel coming down out of heaven, having the key to the Abyss and holding in his hand a great chain. He seized the dragon, that ancient serpent, who is the devil, or Satan, and bound him for a thousand years. He threw him into the Abyss, and locked and sealed it over him, to keep him from deceiving the nations anymore until the thousand years were ended.

—Revelation 20:1-3

The suddenness of the end of the battle of all battles catches all off guard. And, as God had promised, the birds of the air feast at *"the great supper of God."*

And I saw an angel standing in the sun, who cried in a loud voice to all the birds flying in midair, "Come, gather together for the great supper of God, so that you may eat the flesh of kings, generals, and mighty men, of horses and their riders, and the flesh of all people, free and slave, small and great."

—Revelation 19:17-18

Chapter 20

The Procession

> *"They will make war against the Lamb, but the Lamb will overcome them because he is Lord of lords and King of kings—and with him will be his called, chosen and faithful followers."*
>
> —Revelation 17:14 (emphasis added)

With the destruction of the armies of the antichrist, and the hurling of Satan into the Abyss, comes the complete cessation of all fighting. Jesus is triumphant, first at the cross and now on this field of battle—the victory won on the cross now fully manifest before all mankind.

> *Your attitude should be the same as that of Christ Jesus: Who, being in very nature God, did not consider equality with God something to be grasped, but made himself nothing, taking the very nature of a servant, being made in human likeness. And being found in appearance as a man, he humbled himself and became obedient to death—even death on a cross! Therefore God exalted him to the highest place and gave him the name that is above every name, that at the name of Jesus every knee should bow, in heaven and on earth and under the earth, and every tongue confess that Jesus Christ is Lord, to the glory of God the Father.*
>
> —Philippians 2:5-11

The army of *the redeemed* raises their voices in praise to the Victor. The destruction of the armies of the evil one is complete. It is as it had been declared. Jerusalem is now our home. It is where God will live among men.

> *Then you will know that I, the LORD your God, dwell in Zion, my holy hill. Jerusalem will be holy; never again will foreigners invade her.*
>
> —Joel 3:17

All eyes are upon the Lamb. He rides ahead of His army of redemption as we, in formation, parade on the magnificent raised highway past the city gates of Jerusalem. We leave our war machines in the valley east of Jerusalem and join the procession honoring the Lamb Who had been slain.

> *We will shout for joy when you are victorious and will lift up our banners in the name of our God.*
>
> —Psalm 20:5

This is the beginning of all we had hoped for. This is the reign of Jesus throughout the earth. It is a time of great celebration.

> *And a highway will be there; it will be called the Way of Holiness. The unclean will not journey on it; it will be for those who walk in that Way; wicked fools will not go about on it. No lion will be there, nor will any ferocious beast get up on it; they will not be found there. But only the redeemed will walk there, and the ransomed of the LORD will return. They will enter Zion with singing; everlasting joy will crown their heads. Gladness and joy will overtake them, and sorrow and sighing will flee away.*
>
> —Isaiah 35:8-10 (emphasis added)

> *Pass through, pass through the gates! Prepare the way for the people. Build up, build up the highway! Remove the stones. Raise a banner for the nations. The LORD has made proclamation to the ends of the earth: "Say to the Daughter of Zion, 'See, your Savior comes! See, his reward is with him, and his recompense accompanies him.'" They will be called the Holy People, the Redeemed of the LORD; and you will be called Sought After, the City No Longer Deserted.*
>
> —Isaiah 62:10-12).

The entire world now cheers His victory. The triumphant King, mounted on the now blood-spattered white horse, leads His company of warriors—His armies of the Living God—on the highway which courses into the heart of Jerusalem. This is the beginning of the long-awaited reign of *the One*—the Messiah—who had been promised.

> *For to us a child is born, to us a son is given, and the government will be on his shoulders. And he will be called Wonderful Counselor, Mighty God, Everlasting Father, Prince of Peace. Of the increase of*

his government and peace there will be no end. He will reign on David's throne and over his kingdom, establishing and upholding it with justice and righteousness from that time on and forever. The zeal of the LORD Almighty will accomplish this.

—Isaiah 9:6-7

I gaze deep into the eyes of my Friend, my Eternal Companion, my Brother, my Redeemer, my King, my Lord and my God. Jesus looks back with an eternity of love all for me. An eternity.

"The LORD your God is with you, he is mighty to save. He will take great delight in you, he will quiet you with his love, he will rejoice over you with singing."

—Zephaniah 3:17

During my lifetime, the many sightings of *Apache* helicopters had been premonitions of the adventure that I had just experienced. There had been many, many such premonitions of many different varieties. Each of these different premonitions had allowed momentary, alluring flashes of *something deeper* to permeate my life, but only for an instant. As quickly as they had come, they were gone. Their rapid departure left me wondering whether I had really just experienced that which had so captivated my heart.

These were premonitions of incredible beauty, like when I had first laid eyes on my wife's face on that most momentous day; of physical warmth, when I had first held my newborn children; of conquest and accomplishment, when I had watched God heal the incurable; and of sound, when I had first heard the eerie beautiful refrains of *Non Nobis Domine*. These premonitions, which had spoken so plainly of something deep inside me, had awakened previously unknown feelings that had been planted in my heart before time began. They were feelings sown there by a loving God who wanted me to know of the eternity He had planned for me. They were feelings of warmth, of goose bumps, of shivers sent uncontrollably down my spine. They were feelings of eternity, of permanence, of security, of a love that no love on earth could match. They were all eternal and beyond my reach then, but not now.

Each episode—and I realize there had been literally thousands of them during my life—had stirred many responses, mostly emotional. But they all shared a common feeling of eternal anticipation, of something more—much, much more—that was still to come.

After the events of this day, I now know why.

Each had been a foreshadowing of the adventure of eternity that my loving Savior has reserved for me. Before time had begun, the Father, His Son, and their Holy Spirit had known, anticipated, and implemented their sacred, perfect plan for my life—a plan designed to perfectly prepare me for my eternity. The Persons of the Triune God had rejoiced in it, in this perfect plan for my eternal life. The enormity of my God's love for me is overwhelming. The beginning of our eternity together has found its realization in irresistible excitement and adventure in this day of days. And now it continues. It continues with a crescendo, spiraling-upward anticipation, a sensation simply unknown during my life.

The feelings of anticipation of *something more* had always faded away during my life. My futile attempts to restrain their departure likened to grasping water. They had escaped my tightly clasped fingers almost with laughter at the desperation of the futility that swept over me as they simply faded from my awareness. I had not known then what I know now. Now I experience the continually and infinitely accelerating satisfaction of the very deepest longings of my heart. There are so many questions—all centered in my utter amazement of the eternity before me.

How can these feelings of satisfaction continue to accelerate so? They are blowing my hair back! How can there be satisfaction but no satiation, no saturation? There has to be an end! There always was during my life. There has to be a maximum point at which it will all end. For how can I maintain this level of simultaneous desire and fulfillment of that desire—let alone continue to accelerate in both? It is an overpowering feeling. And in such is found the very definition of that ever-so-holy word *infinite.* It was undefinable, unimaginable during my life. My limited human mind could not envision something that it had simply never experienced, for nothing in my life had been infinite. And yet now that word defines everything. *Infinite* is the very nature of God. It defines every one of His attributes. My eternity is with God; my eternity is in the infinite God.

And yet in all of this I am still very much *Nathaniel.* I will remain Nathaniel for eternity. The very nature of my *"yes"* to the question that God asked in my sophomore year in college, whether or not my response was truly *free*—truly an exercise of unrestrained free will—is simply no longer a necessary topic of discussion. The question regarding the nature of *free* choice, whether or not it is really free, and whether my fate had been pre-ordained by God as one of the *"predestined,"* the *"elect,"* or the *"chosen"* no longer matters. It is no longer relevant. I am joyfully and amazingly still Nathaniel. I inhabit a physical body. It is mine for eternity. I am very much *alive,* as it had never been defined during my life. My eternity will be in the exploration of the Living God. I am so indebted to this God that I love. That which I know for sure is that I, Nathaniel, bring nothing to eternity except that which is found in my Savior, the only Son of God, Jesus.

And eternity – wow! There is no question of "running out of things to do." For I am finite created man, contained entirely in and exploring forever, the infinite uncreated God. The only amount of time that can be adequate to approach this unreachable goal is precisely that which has been granted me by my merciful God—*an eternity*. Such is, only by the grace of God, the eternal capability of my awesomely created heart, which now belongs wholly and only and joyfully to Jesus.

> *One thing I ask of the LORD, this is what I seek: that I may dwell in the house of the LORD all the days of my life, to gaze upon the beauty of the LORD and to seek him in his temple.*
>
> —Psalm 27:4

www.ingramcontent.com/pod-product-compliance
Lightning Source LLC
Chambersburg PA
CBHW070528030426
42337CB00016B/2155